TIES, RAILS, and TELEGRAPH WIRES

Photographer unknown, MHS, PAc 2013-50.1242

This view across a border of nations and railways in the mid-1910s looks north from the Great Northern Railway property in Sweet Grass, Montana, into the Canadian Pacific Railway yard in Coutts, Alberta. Straddling the border are the station, which housed both railway and customs functions, and the platform. The Canadian Pacific train has reached the end of its southbound run from Lethbridge.

TIES, RAILS, and TELEGRAPH WIRES

Railroads and Communities in Montana and the West

DALE MARTIN

MONTANA HISTORICAL SOCIETY PRESS
Helena

Front cover photograph (color tinting added): A Northern Pacific eastbound extra freight nears the west portal of the tunnel under Bozeman Pass, between Bozeman and Livingston, on a cold February 10, 1939. Both the lead locomotive and the helper engine pushing at the rear end of the train are sending upward great plumes of condensing steam. The middle of the train is passing the little railway community of West End, the location of a telegraph station and track maintenance section base. Warren McGee, photographer, MHS Photographic Archives, Helena, PAc 97-93.2344

Back cover photograph: Looking east toward North Dakota from the top of the Milwaukee Road's water tank at Baker, Montana, in about 1910, shortly after the completion of its extension from South Dakota to Puget Sound. The tracks are, right to left: the main line, a long passing siding, a yard track, and an industry track, along which are grain elevators and the freight house. Between the photographer and the passenger depot are a shed-roofed coal house and gable-roofed privy, with lattice entry enclosure. The platted streets, not yet fully delineated, on each side of the railway corridor, are Milwaukee Avenue on the north side (left) and Railroad Avenue on the south side (right). The north end of the business district is on the right. Photographer unknown, MHS Photographic Archives, Helena, PAc 83-33.3

Cover and book design by Diane Gleba Hall
Typeset in Warnock Pro and Grotesque
Printed in the United States

18 19 20 21 22 23 24 10 9 8 7 6 5 4 3 2 1

978-1-9405279-3-2 (cloth)
978-1-9405279-2-5 (paper)

Library of Congress Cataloging-in-Publication Data
Names: Martin, Dale, author.
Title: Ties, rails, and telegraph wires : railroads and communities in Montana and the West / by Dale Martin.
Description: First edition. | Helena, Montana : Montana Historical Society Press, [2017] | Includes bibliographical references and index.
Identifiers: LCCN 2017061209| ISBN 9781940527925 (softcover) | ISBN 9781940527932 (hardcover)
Subjects: LCSH: Railroads—Social aspects—Montana—History. | Railroads—Social aspects—Rocky Mountains Region—History. | City and town life—Montana—History. | City and town life—Rocky Mountains Region—History. | Montana—History, Local. | Rocky Mountains Region—History, Local.
Classification: LCC HE2771.M9 M37 2017 | DDC 385.09786—dc23

THE MONTANA HISTORICAL SOCIETY gratefully acknowledges the financial support provided for this publication by

Wilda Bell Memorial

BNSF Railway Foundation

Center for Western Lands and Peoples at
Montana State University–Bozeman

Elise R. Donahue Charitable Trust

Friends of the Society

Estate of Patricia Hoksbergen

LIATIS Foundation

Montana Department of Transportation

Charlotte Thomas Memorial

Linda Sandman

Courtesy the author

At Billings Union Station on July 9, 1967, the author's parents, sister, and brother stand next to a member of the train crew before boarding the Burlington Route's three-car train to Denver.

This book is dedicated to my parents, who took my brother, sister, and me to many railroad stations and onto many trains.

I grew up along the Great Northern main line on the North Dakota prairie, where the only connections to the rest of the world were the track and the telegraph.

—KEN C. BROVALD, "Recollections of an Omaha Brasspounder"

Contents

Acknowledgments

MANY people contributed to the completion of this book, enough to fill most of a day coach on a local train over a half century ago.

Ties, Rails, and Telegraph Wires is the product of several converging factors, some going back decades. The earliest influence is my riding the last of the great passenger trains in the 1960s with my family. At that time, I began to accumulate paper materials on railroads, first for hobby collecting and then anticipating their use in research. During a road trip in 2000, Mark Fiege encouraged me to write a book about railroads in the human landscape of the West.

The institutional beginning of this book lies with two state agencies, the Montana Historical Society (MHS) and the Montana Department of Transportation (MDT). In 2012, the MHS's State Historic Preservation Office and MDT, representing the Federal Highway Administration, executed a programmatic agreement under the National Historic Preservation Act to address recurrent impacts from federally funded highway projects to abandoned railroad grades in Montana, a class of historic properties considered eligible for listing in the National Register of Historic Places. As partial mitigation for these impacts, MDT agreed to help fund the publication of a Montana Historical Society Press book about Montana's railroad history. This book serves in fulfillment of that purpose and agreement.

Several people at or associated with the Montana Historical Society provided crucial assistance and support in the creation of this book. Editor Molly Holz encouraged me as I developed the subject of railways, stations, and trains in the lives of people and communities. Glenda Bradshaw came out of retirement to work as the book's photo editor. She found many photos to complement the text and diligently pursued use permissions for images. Copyeditor Jo Ann Reece helped me iron out particulars, and Diane Gleba Hall designed the book. Photo archivist Jeff Malcomson helped me find photographs in the Warren McGee Collection. MHS volunteer Gerry Daumiller made the maps. He was patient and responsive as I suggested changes and alterations through many draft revisions.

Jon Axline, historian at the Montana Department of Transportation, represented MDT with its generous funding of and institutional interest in the project. He also made arrangements for the MHS Press to use MDT's copy of the historic Great Northern Railway plat of Zurich, Montana.

Much of the material for this book is drawn from my own collection of files, papers, and publications. Research took me frequently to the library at Montana State University–Bozeman (MSU), where Jan Zauha searches tenaciously on behalf of historians. The bound volumes of newspapers of the Butte-Silver Bow Public Archives, where Ellen Crain is director, are truly enjoyable to use, something few would say of any microforms.

Several people read the entire manuscript and offered valuable suggestions. The text benefited greatly from early readings by Michelle Maskiell and Susan Cohen. The Montana Historical Society Press's outside readers, Fred Quivik, Carlos Schwantes, and Jon Axline, added useful comments. Mary Murphy read it with her advocacy for vivid and clear wording. Early in the work, a seminar organized by Jennifer Dunn and Amanda Hardin in the MSU Department of History and Philosophy provided the first opportunity for me to present themes and stories to others.

Numerous people contributed to finding photographs for the book. Many of the photos are in the collections of the Museum of the Rockies in Bozeman, available online, where Steve Jackson, curator of art and photography, offered full cooperation. Rachel Phillips, research coordinator at the Gallatin History Museum, also in Bozeman, found photos based on my written description of the scenes portrayed. Megan Sanford at The History Museum in Great Falls found a photo in that institution's collection. David Hull, of Helena, provided two photos from his collection.

Some others generously responded to requests for permission to use photographs and images. Shirley Burman-Steinheimer allowed me to use a sequence of photos taken by Richard Steinheimer. David

Plowden gave permission for a photo now in the collection of the Beinecke Library at Yale University. Bill Wyckoff allowed use of a photo from his fieldwork. Kevin EuDaly at White River Productions allowed the use of the cover of a *Railroad Magazine*. The Newberry Library provided a photo taken during a project sponsored by the Burlington Route in 1948. LaTrelle Scherffius shared her knowledge of the collection of photos by Robert C. Morrison of Miles City, now in the collections of the Montana Historical Society.

Requests for information were answered by Rufus Cone, Mark Hufstetler, and Emmett Moore Jr. For frequent support and encouragement from those not mentioned above, I owe thanks to Billy Smith, David Large, Kristen Intemann, Bob Rydell, Mitzi Rossillon, and Simon Dixon. And special appreciation to Brad Snow and Mike McManus, founders of the MSU instructors' monthly seminar, with beer, at the hospitable Colombo's Pizza & Pasta in Bozeman.

The Department of History and Philosophy at Montana State University–Bozeman provided valuable logistical support, with both equipment and help using it, which was necessary for an author immersed in the era of steam.

And I thank my family: Mary Murphy likes, most of the time, trains, and still misses the caboose at the end of a freight train. She values, all the time, good writing and people's stories. This book benefited from her constant support and advocacy of both of those preferences.

My parents—Dale and Leila Martin—made railroads and trains, with meals in the dining car, part of childhood for my brother Eric, sister Val, and me. They also taught the three of us to value books, history, and getting out to see historic landscapes, even in the rain. For these reasons, the book is dedicated to my parents.

Absaroka Mountains, Montana, Gustav Krollmann, c. 1930, Northern Pacific Railway

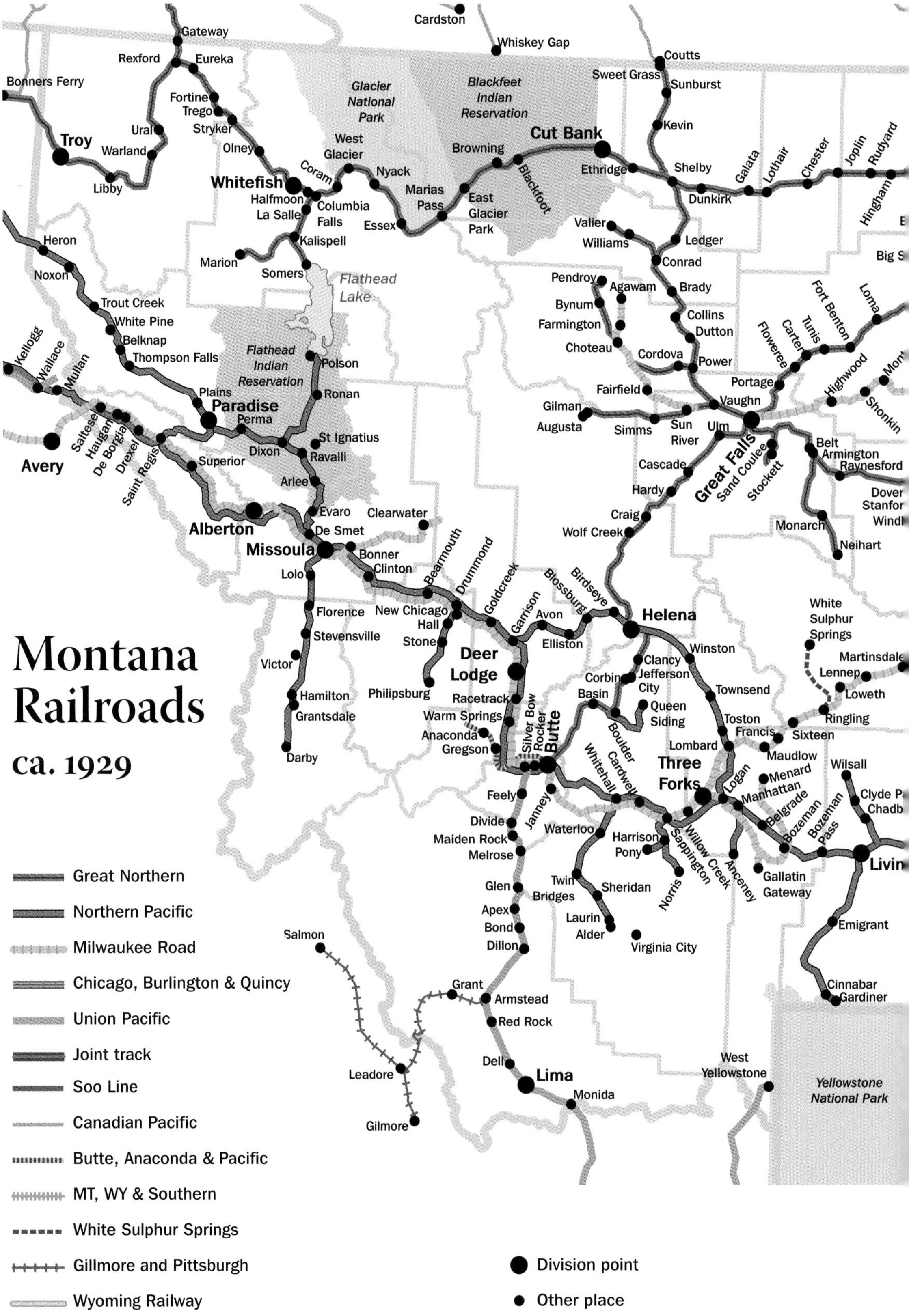
Montana Railroads
ca. 1929
Great Northern
Northern Pacific
Milwaukee Road
Chicago, Burlington & Quincy
Union Pacific
Joint track
Soo Line
Canadian Pacific
Butte, Anaconda & Pacific
MT, WY & Southern
White Sulphur Springs
Gillmore and Pittsburgh
Wyoming Railway
Division point
Other place
Glacier National Park
Blackfeet Indian Reservation
Flathead Indian Reservation
Flathead Lake
Yellowstone National Park
Cardston
Whiskey Gap
Coutts
Sweet Grass
Sunburst
Kevin
Gateway
Rexford
Eureka
Bonners Ferry
Fortine
Trego
Stryker
Ural
Troy
Warland
Libby
Olney
Whitefish
Halfmoon
La Salle
Coram
Columbia Falls
Kalispell
Marion
Somers
West Glacier
Nyack
Essex
Marias Pass
Browning
East Glacier Park
Blackfoot
Cut Bank
Ethridge
Shelby
Dunkirk
Galata
Lothair
Chester
Joplin
Rudyard
Hingham
Big S
Valier
Williams
Ledger
Conrad
Brady
Pendroy
Agawam
Bynum
Farmington
Choteau
Collins
Dutton
Cordova
Power
Fairfield
Portage
Vaughn
Gilman
Augusta
Simms
Sun River
Ulm
Great Falls
Sand Coulee
Stockett
Cascade
Hardy
Craig
Wolf Creek
Fort Benton
Loma
Floweree
Carter
Tunis
Highwood
Shonkin
Belt
Armington
Raynesford
Dover
Stanfor
Windh
Monarch
Neihart
Heron
Noxon
Trout Creek
White Pine
Belknap
Thompson Falls
Plains
Paradise
Perma
Kellogg
Wallace
Mullan
Saltese
Haugan
De Borgia
Drexel
Saint Regis
Avery
Superior
Alberton
Polson
Ronan
St Ignatius
Ravalli
Dixon
Arlee
Evaro
De Smet
Clearwater
Missoula
Bonner
Clinton
Bearmouth
Drummond
Goldcreek
Garrison
Avon
Elliston
Blossburg
Birdseye
Helena
Lolo
Florence
Stevensville
Victor
Hamilton
Grantsdale
Darby
New Chicago
Hall
Stone
Philipsburg
Deer Lodge
Racetrack
Warm Springs
Anaconda
Gregson
Silver Bow
Rocker
Butte
Clancy
Jefferson City
Corbin
Basin
Queen Siding
Boulder
Winston
Townsend
Toston
Lombard
Three Forks
Whitehall
Cardwell
Janney
Feely
Divide
Maiden Rock
Melrose
Waterloo
Harrison
Pony
Sappington
Willow Creek
Norris
Anceney
Logan
Manhattan
Menard
Maudlow
Belgrade
Bozeman
Bozeman Pass
Gallatin Gateway
Francis
Sixteen
Ringling
White Sulphur Springs
Martinsdale
Lennep
Loweth
Wilsall
Clyde P
Chadb
Livin
Emigrant
Cinnabar
Gardiner
Glen
Apex
Bond
Dillon
Twin Bridges
Sheridan
Laurin
Alder
Virginia City
Salmon
Grant
Armstead
Red Rock
Leadore
Gilmore
Dell
Lima
Monida
West Yellowstone

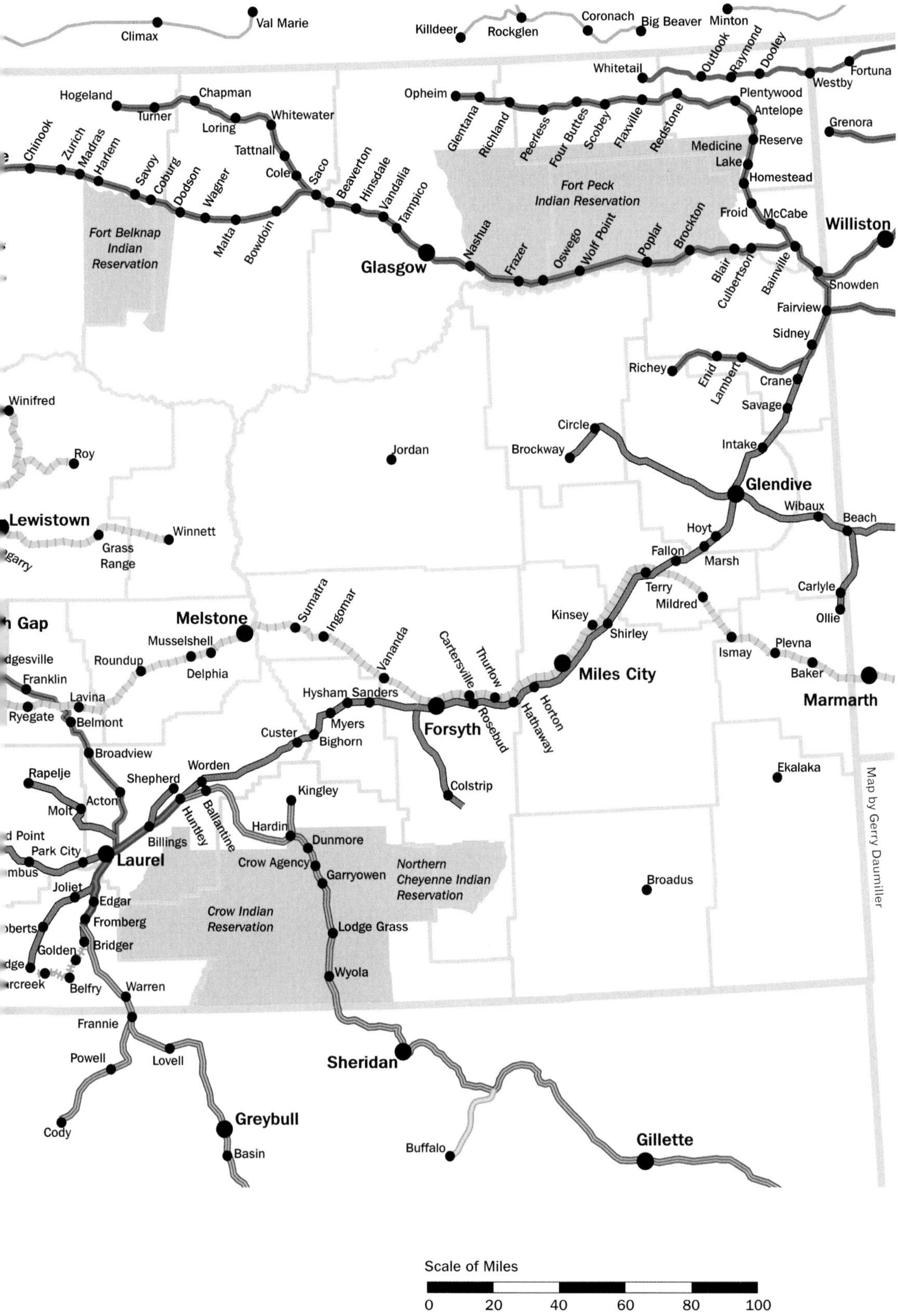
Climax
Val Marie
Killdeer
Rockglen
Coronach
Big Beaver
Minton
Outlook
Raymond
Dooley
Whitetail
Westby
Fortuna
Grenora
Hogeland
Turner
Chapman
Loring
Whitewater
Tattnall
Cole
Saco
Opheim
Glentana
Richland
Peerless
Four Buttes
Scobey
Flaxville
Redstone
Plentywood
Antelope
Reserve
Medicine Lake
Homestead
Froid
McCabe
Williston
Chinook
Zurich
Madras
Harlem
Savoy
Coburg
Dodson
Wagner
Malta
Bowdoin
Beaverton
Hinsdale
Vandalia
Tampico
Fort Belknap Indian Reservation
Fort Peck Indian Reservation
Glasgow
Nashua
Frazer
Oswego
Wolf Point
Poplar
Brockton
Blair
Culbertson
Bainville
Snowden
Fairview
Sidney
Richey
Enid
Lambert
Crane
Savage
Winifred
Roy
Jordan
Circle
Brockway
Intake
Glendive
Wibaux
Beach
Lewistown
Winnett
Grass Range
Hoyt
Fallon
Marsh
Terry
Mildred
Carlyle
Ollie
Kinsey
Shirley
Ismay
Plevna
Baker
Marmarth
Melstone
Sumatra
Ingomar
Musselshell
Roundup
Delphia
Vananda
Cartersville
Thurlow
Miles City
Horton
Hathaway
Rosebud
Forsyth
Hysham
Sanders
Myers
Bighorn
Custer
Franklin
Lavina
Ryegate
Belmont
Broadview
Worden
Shepherd
Rapelje
Acton
Molt
Huntley
Ballantine
Billings
Laurel
Park City
Kingley
Colstrip
Hardin
Dunmore
Crow Agency
Garryowen
Northern Cheyenne Indian Reservation
Ekalaka
Joliet
Edgar
Fromberg
Bridger
Golden
Belfry
Warren
Crow Indian Reservation
Lodge Grass
Wyola
Broadus
Frannie
Powell
Lovell
Cody
Greybull
Basin
Sheridan
Buffalo
Gillette
Map by Gerry Daumiller
Scale of Miles
0
20
40
60
80
100

Railroad Advertising Art

In the late nineteenth and early twentieth centuries, railroads heavily advertised their premier passenger trains and the destinations those trains served. Among the main visual forms of publicity were eye-catching images printed on posters. Good-quality reproductions of colorful paintings were far more striking than black-and-white photographs, and this era of railroad promotion coincided with technical innovations in commercial printing that made possible the inexpensive mass printing of large multihued posters. The railroads placed posters in many of their own depots and ticket offices, as well as hotels and other businesses that the public frequented. Railways commissioned well-known artists to paint scenes either visible from trains or reached by rail, and in some views trains were shown in the scenery. Canyons, mountains, lakes, and coasts were favorite subjects, and the wonders of national parks received extensive coverage. A few railroads featured the Native Americans who lived on reservations along the rail lines. The painted images appeared on large posters and on smaller items, such as wall calendars, brochures, timetables, menus, postcards, and playing cards that were widely distributed.

Several railroads serving Montana invested heavily in art for publicity. The Northern Pacific hired Gustav Krollmann, born and raised in Vienna, to paint scenes

North Coast Limited in the Montana Rockies, Gustav Krollmann, c. 1930, Northern Pacific Railway

Montana Historical Society Museum, Haynes Foundation Collection, Gift of Mrs. Isabel Haynes, John Reddy, photographer, 1980.61.155

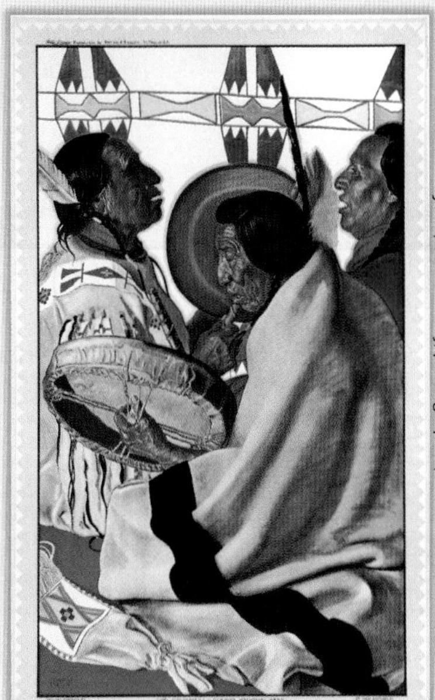

Drummers Buffalo Body, Heavy Breast, and Sure Chief, 1933, reproduced from *The Drummers*, by Winold Reiss, Great Northern Railway

Montana Historical Society Museum, Haynes Foundation Collection, Gift of Mrs. Isabel Haynes, John Reddy, photographer, 1980.61.221

of the northern Rockies and the Cascade Range. He often showed the company's passenger trains, with smoke swept back by speed, before a background of Montana's mountains. After the creation of Glacier National Park in 1910, Great Northern's art particularly focused on that park. The railway's art also featured the Blackfeet Indians from the reservation on the east side of Glacier. The GN engaged several men and women, including German immigrant portrait specialist Winold Reiss and Montana native Elizabeth Lochrie, to paint the park's scenery and many Blackfeet individuals. Union Pacific's art emphasized Yellowstone National Park, reached by its line through Idaho to West Yellowstone.

Railroads also issued publicity with colorful illustrations to draw settlers to areas believed to have high potential for agricultural development. The companies particularly wanted homesteaders to settle on public lands along rail lines, and then ship the products of their farms on freight trains. Idealized images of prosperous farms, smiling clean farmers, and the rich produce of farms appeared on posters and on the covers of brochures with advice to prospective settlers.

Yellowstone National Park, 11596

Yellowstone National Park, artist unidentified, 1923, Union Pacific Railroad

Montana Historical Society Library, PAM 3882

"Montana," Chicago, Milwaukee and St. Paul Railway

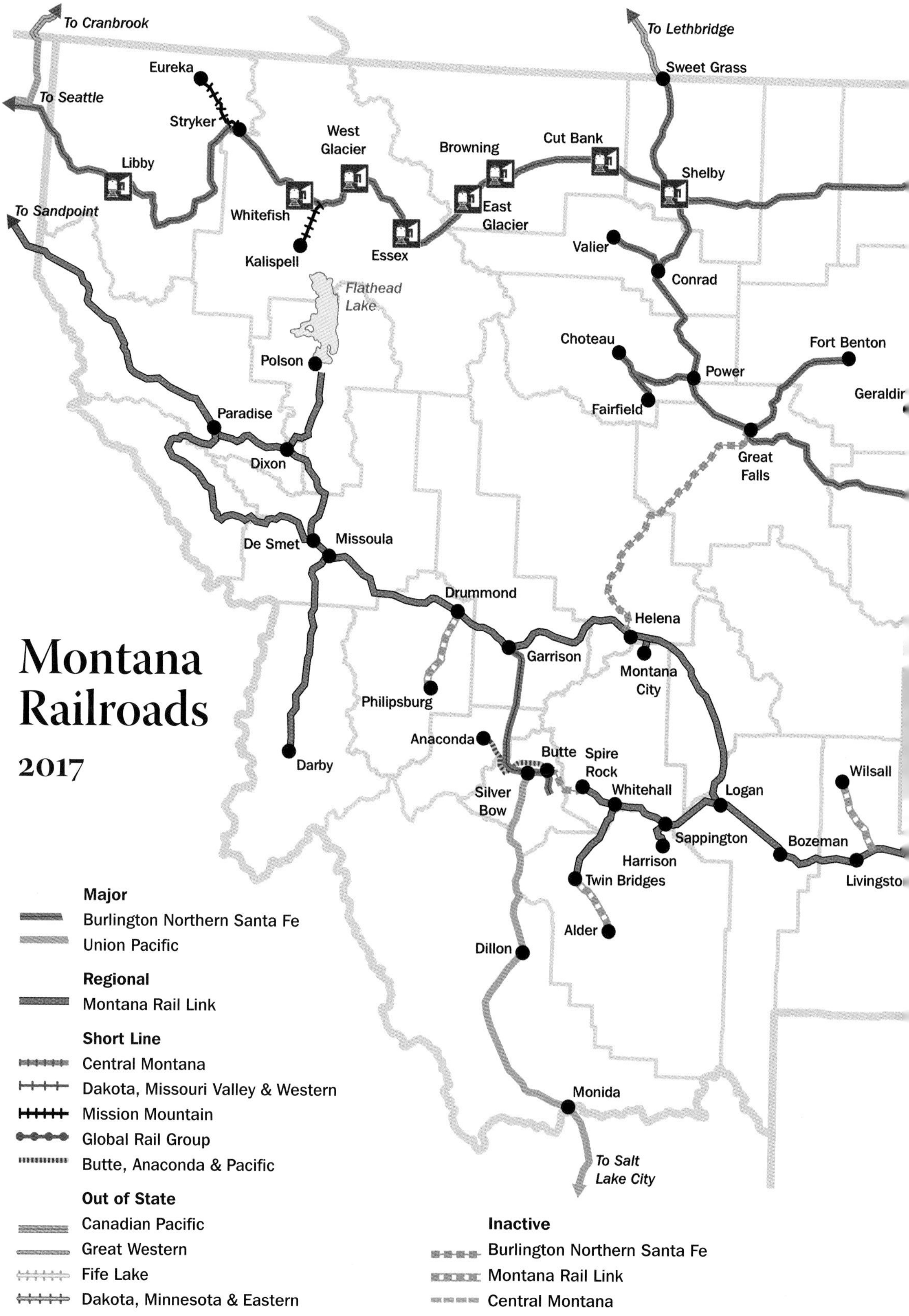
Montana Railroads
2017
To Cranbrook
To Seattle
To Sandpoint
To Lethbridge
To Salt Lake City
Eureka
Stryker
Libby
Whitefish
Kalispell
West Glacier
Essex
Browning
East Glacier
Cut Bank
Sweet Grass
Shelby
Valier
Conrad
Flathead Lake
Polson
Choteau
Fairfield
Power
Fort Benton
Geraldir
Great Falls
Paradise
Dixon
De Smet
Missoula
Darby
Drummond
Philipsburg
Garrison
Helena
Montana City
Anaconda
Butte
Silver Bow
Spire Rock
Whitehall
Logan
Sappington
Harrison
Twin Bridges
Alder
Dillon
Monida
Bozeman
Livingsto
Wilsall
Major
Burlington Northern Santa Fe
Union Pacific
Regional
Montana Rail Link
Short Line
Central Montana
Dakota, Missouri Valley & Western
Mission Mountain
Global Rail Group
Butte, Anaconda & Pacific
Out of State
Canadian Pacific
Great Western
Fife Lake
Dakota, Minnesota & Eastern
Inactive
Burlington Northern Santa Fe
Montana Rail Link
Central Montana

Climax
Bracken
To Moose Jaw
Coronach
To Flaxton
Whitetail
Westby
Scobey
Plentywood
Malta
Glasgow
Wolf Point
Bainville
Williston
To Chicago
Snowden
Fairview
Sidney
Crane
Fort Peck Lake
Circle
ing Creek
ction
Lewistown
Glendive
Wibaux
To Minneapolis
Terry
Miles City
Baker
To Minneapolis
Bull Mountain
Sanders
Forsyth
Broadview
Huntley
Colstrip
Absaloka Mine
Mossmain
Billings
Laurel
Map by Gerry Daumiller
Decker
Colony
Frannie
Sheridan
To Rapid City
Cody
Greybull
Gillette
To Colorado and Texas
To Shawnee Jct
To Nebraska
Amtrak station
Other place
Scale of Miles
0
20
40
60
80
100

Yellowstone National Park, 11594

Where Gush the Geysers, artist unidentified, 1921, Oregon Short Line

Montana Historical Society Library, PAM 3757

"Montana Free Homestead Land," Great Northern

Montana Historical Society Library, PAM 850

"With the Mountaineers in Glacier National Park," Great Northern

Montana Historical Society Library, PAM 4105

"Apple Talk," Northern Pacific

Introduction

Ringling, Montana

THE NOTABLE Montana writer Ivan Doig revisited the small town of Ringling in central Montana in July 1983. He had lived there during parts of his childhood in the 1940s and 1950s, and many members of his extended family still lived in the area. Doig noticed the crew that was dismantling the track of the bankrupt Milwaukee Road's transcontinental main line, over which the last trains ran in March 1980. As a youth, he had watched trains on that track, and he rode on trains during a time of significant transition in his life. "Change is one thing," he wrote, "but diminution is radically another. It made me want to go to the depot, as when I was twenty, and summon the Milwaukee into creation once again."[1]

Doig may have been thinking of a daily event in the several years up to 1958, when about lunch time, if they were on schedule, two streamlined passenger trains pulled by electric engines paused briefly in Ringling. The westbound and eastbound editions of the *Olympian Hiawatha* were near midway on their journeys between Chicago and Seattle-Tacoma. The *Olympian Hiawatha* represented the multiple functions and accommodations of a premier main line passenger train at that time. Passengers rode in coaches and sleepers, with meals and beverages available in the dining car, lounge, and parlor car. In the cars at the head end of the train were a mobile post office and space for bags of mail, railway express, and other priority shipments, including milk, coffins, and newspapers.[2] It was a thousand-foot-long multipurpose conveyance and a link to the world beyond Meagher County and central Montana. Whether

Ron V. Nixon, photographer, MOR RVN 26138

The view eastward from the platform of the Milwaukee Road station at Ringling on May 20, 1962, about the time Ivan Doig finished his university education that had required regular train rides between Ringling and Chicago, which decades later he fondly recalled in memoirs. Approaching the station (center right) is a short passenger train, the Minneapolis–Deer Lodge remnant of the *Olympian Hiawatha*—the Chicago to Seattle-Tacoma service that ended one year earlier. On the left, an eastbound extra freight train waits on the passing siding. Its two electric engines were built in the United States just after World War II for Soviet railways, but growing Cold War tensions prevented their delivery. The Milwaukee Road acquired twelve of them, and the crews called them "Little Joes," a reference to Josef Stalin.

Ron V. Nixon, photographer, MOR RVN 21861

The *Olympian Hiawatha* waits at the Deer Lodge division point for a crew change on March 28, 1958. Ivan Doig remembered that when a Milwaukee passenger train pulled by an electric locomotive stopped at Ringling, the engine "hummed there in orange and black grandeur." This distinctive "bipolar" engine (named for the type of electric motor inside) was almost at the end of nearly forty years of operation and would soon be replaced by a diesel-electric. Just behind the engine is the Railway Post Office portion of the mail-express car. Today, engine E-2 is preserved at a St. Louis railroad museum.

seen or ridden, nothing on north-south U.S. Route 89 at the east edge of town could match the *Olympian Hiawatha.*

Between 1957 and 1962, Doig studied at Northwestern University in Evanston, just north of Chicago. For most of that time, he seasonally rode the *Olympian Hiawatha* between Ringling and Chicago. He recalled:

> [I]t was a royal feeling to be the only person getting on or off a train when it stopped in Ringling. For those few minutes you commanded the entire great power chain of the railroad. Trainmen, section crews, depot agent paused in their day because you were of Ringling. The engine hummed there in orange and black grandeur while you placed your foot on the metal step of ascent or descent. The whole dauntless trellis of ties and rails between Chicago and Ringling had been created for this.[3]

Doig recalled the valuable time for observation and reflection available on trains. The many hours over long distances "were the enforced pause in time when . . . I could count the steps taken in the college year and those still to come."[4]

More quickly and completely than on competing main lines in the West, the diminution of the Milwaukee Road through Ringling began around the time Doig ended his seasonal trips to Chicago. In 1961, the Milwaukee Road replaced the *Olympian Hiawatha* with a smaller train over a shorter run between Minneapolis and Deer Lodge, Montana, an operation federally mandated to serve towns (like Ringling) with no alternative transport. This train ran less than three years. Operation of electric locomotives in Montana stopped in 1974. The Milwaukee itself went bankrupt in 1977 and three years later ceased operations across most of Montana.[5]

In the second half of the twentieth century, Ringling was one of thousands of towns that lost passenger and other rail services, railroad jobs, and the familiar presence of trains that had always been a part of the townscape. A historian of railway decline and abandonment notes:

> The emotional impact of the closing of rail lines in small communities is a poignant, largely undocumented, part of the American railroad saga. For older residents, the loss can be a sad and unwelcome reminder of the ways in which everyday life has changed. . . .

Ron V. Nixon, photographer, MOR RVN 33139

The Milwaukee Road division point of Alberton, thirty-two miles west of Missoula, was a crew change location from 1909 until March 1980, when the railroad ended all operations west of eastern Montana. Five months later, on August 6, Ron Nixon captured the early appearance of abandonment: boarded-up station windows and rust accumulating on the rails of the main line and switchyard.

> Even for those who do not have a personal connection to trains, the sight of abandoned railroad corridors in the process of being reclaimed by weeds and trees often stirs profound reactions. Evoking images of the powerful market forces that pushed once mighty transportation companies toward oblivion, these routes are reminders of how the work of entire generations can be discarded with the advent of new technology or business practices.[6]

The Railway World

Ties, Rails, and Telegraph Wires explores North American communities that were thoroughly connected and daily served by a network of trains, stations, and railroaders. The story's focus in time and region is the first two-thirds of the twentieth century in Montana and the West, the Midwest, and Canada. It covers the decades of established and thorough services for residents and businesses in towns and cities that relied almost entirely upon railways for transportation beyond their locale. The emphasis is on stations and the business of passenger trains and, to a lesser extent, on the local freights with which the railways served their business customers in thousands of places. Tens of millions of people counted on this rail system for travel, carriage of express and mail, and the transportation of food, consumer goods, and virtually all of the other necessities of life. And the sights and sounds of trains, usually unnoticed until they were almost gone, provided the daily background of the community fabric, linking fellow citizens by work and travel. The memories that feature trains—excerpts from novels and short stories, movies, and music lyrics—convey railways as aspects of both everyday life and special events that emerge in retrospect as images and experiences worthy of recall.

Railroads provided the most extensive network of scheduled intercity transportation that ever existed in North America. During the decades between the end of the main era of transcontinental railway construction (mid-1890s) and the rising prominence of motor vehicles (1920s), railways offered a greater range of transportation and associated communications services than any single mode of mechanical transport either before or since. In the United States, "at their peak just before the First World War, 98 percent of all intercity travel was by rail. No other means of transportation, not even the automobile, has achieved such a monopoly."[7] Railroads provided the first fast, inexpensive, reliable, all-weather services for passengers, express, mail, and freight to tens of thousands of communities.

The great range of services once provided almost entirely by railways is now shared with airlines, buses, trucking firms, parcel delivery companies, and even telecommunications firms. But during that era, trains met nearly all land transportation needs beyond local travel. Scheduled passenger trains carried individuals and families traveling distances ranging from within a county to across the country as well as U.S. mail, priority express, and occasionally unusual passengers, such as racehorses. Unscheduled "extra" trains were operated for groups attending national conventions, transporting military recruits to mobilization points, and for traveling shows. At the edge of land, the railways connected to scheduled steamboats and ferryboats on lakes, saltwater inlets, bays, and along coasts. In Montana during the early twentieth century, for example, steamboats on Flathead Lake met trains at Somers in the north and Polson in the south. Freight trains carried less-than-carload (LCL) shipments, such as furniture and machinery parts, perishable foodstuffs in refrigerated cars, and carload freight like lumber, livestock, and coal. Besides providing railway

A Great Northern passenger train stands at the railway's Helena passenger station on October 10, 1941. The white metal flags at the front of the locomotive indicate it is an extra train. Photographer Ron Nixon wrote in his caption: "What makes this train unusual is that many of the passengers, riding in the unusual cars [the first three cars] at the head end of the train, are horses. They are race horses headed to Calgary, Alberta." The GN took the train to the Canadian border at Sweet Grass–Coutts and the Canadian Pacific Railway the rest of the way to its destination.

Ron V. Nixon, photographer, MOR RVN 11488

communications, the wires on the telegraph pole lines next to the tracks also carried commercial traffic for companies like Western Union and news organizations.

Railway transportation was an essential component of the landscape of North America during this time. Their tracks, trains, and employees were constant visual, aural, and smoky reminders of the transport system that kept the economy going. In thousands of cities, towns, and small communities, the railway station, where the railroad retailed its business, offered a close and familiar portal between the local economy and the continental network of commerce.

In the late nineteenth and early twentieth centuries, railroad operations and properties in Montana were part of a standardized interconnected rail network spanning North America from maritime eastern Canada to the Mexican border with Guatemala. There was a similarity in the design, materials, and appearance of tracks, stations, bridges, telegraph pole lines, locomotive roundhouses, and the freight and passenger cars throughout the continent, in contrast to their visibly different counterparts in Europe or Asia.

Many of the towns and cities in the West and Midwest owed their creation, growth, and expectations of long prosperity to this new transport system. The railroad's modern transport stood in stark contrast to local travel—on foot, by horse, or in horse-drawn vehicles—that remained far more limited in scope and speed. The steam engines revolutionizing long-distance transportation in the nineteenth century were too large and mechanically sensitive to be used in small personal vehicles on the rough roads of the time. Most people continued to travel locally as they had for centuries, on foot or by horse. Electric streetcar lines ran in some towns and cities, but these were scarcer in the interior West than throughout much of the nation.

The strengths and limits of rail travel were evident in service between neighboring towns. Depending on the frequency and timing of scheduled trains, a round-trip to a town fifteen miles away could take part of a day or require an overnight stay. Throughout this time period, the businesses in each town tried to provide diversity and self-sufficiency. Towns and cities were compact, walkable places where for most people their residence, work, shopping, errands, entertainment, worship, and celebration were all close together.

The transportation system, which combined a national network of steam railroads and local travel by horse, shaped rural landscapes of towns and farms that were as full of visible human labor and enterprise as they would ever be. People lived close to their work of growing, extracting, storing, processing, and shipping the products of farms, ranches, forests, and mines. Operations situated away from towns needed to operate residential camps for loggers, miners, and even workers at dams. In towns, the central role of railroads was evident in the steam engines shunting freight cars on spur tracks next to grain elevators, flour mills, stockyards, wool warehouses, sawmills, manufacturing plants, lumber and coal yards, breweries, wholesale firms, and the "house track" next to the station where less-than-carload freight was delivered.

Many of the hopeful townspeople and the farmers who shopped in town believed that their investment—not just in money but in a combination of long hours, risk of failure, physical toil, rural isolation, and times of deprivation—was building a world that would last for generations. Merchants invested in buildings and equipment with the assumption that they would have decades of prosperity as the primary market for the surrounding and growing rural population. In 1915, the new owner and editor of a newspaper arrived in the small plains town of Flagler, Colorado. His son later recalled his father announcing to those at the Rock Island Railway station that he was staying, "'The rest of my life,' Father said. 'All the rest of my life.'"[8]

The first motor vehicles were seen as a replacement for horses but not a threat to the business of railways. Hal Borland wrote of horse-and-wagon travel on country roads, on the plains of northeastern Colorado, in the late 1910s: "The automobile was going to change all that, but we didn't yet know it. We merely thought that the Model T was a mechanical wonder—which it was—and that with it we could break a few of the bonds of time and distance, but only a few." This was especially true in the winter.

> The roads, still designed primarily for horse-drawn vehicles, were plowed open or a track was shoveled through the deepest drifts only where the snow was belly-deep on a horse. If the wind drifted an opened road full overnight, it was up to the next traveler to find a way through or around. Travel beyond the immediate vicinity of a town was by rail, and the Rock Island [Railway] had a rotary plow out clearing the rails after every storm.[9]

For several decades after the 1910s, even as the popularity and usage of motor vehicles grew, railroads continued to run passenger trains on an extensive network. At midcentury, one could ride a train to Danvers, Montana, a small town northwest of Lewistown located on a secondary line of the Milwaukee Road. Until 1955, the Milwaukee operated a pair of short passenger trains between the transcontinental main line at Harlowton, through Lewistown, and Great Falls. These daily trains stopped at the staffed station in Danvers.

Nearly sixty years after her aunt rode the train to and from Danvers, Mary Clearman Blew wrote of the changes in travel choices in those decades. Her aunt, Imogene Welch, was a schoolteacher south of Olympia, Washington, during the Second World War. In late May 1943, Welch returned to her family home near Danvers. Blew noted:

> Another sign of the times. On the one hand, she can't drive back to Montana in her car, because gasoline is being rationed and she doesn't have enough gasoline coupons. On the other hand, the public transportation available to her in the 1940s is enviable. She can get anywhere in the Pacific northwest by train or bus, even to places like Danvers, Montana, which has only a general store, a saloon, and a couple of grain elevators in addition to its train station.[10]

Transportation, experienced as well as observed, has often been a portal for recall and assessment of the past. It is an evocative way to hold and organize memories, whether in daily life and work or in unusual episodes, such as leaving home for college or military service. For an individual, it might be a memory of a first or favorite car, the train regularly ridden on holiday family visits, or the name of an ocean liner taken on a rare journey between continents. For a community, it might be Main Street, which was also a numbered U.S. route through town. There, one could see license plates from many states. Where there is water, it might be the ferry system that carried passengers and vehicles to work or favorite weekend destinations. Remember, there was a time when air travel was relatively new, unusual, and something that people anticipated with pleasure.

One resident of Bozeman, on the main line of the Northern Pacific Railway (NP) across southern Montana, recalled both

Warren McGee, photographer, MHS, PAc 97-93.7658

On March 17, 1946, Warren McGee caught the Milwaukee Road's westbound Harlowton–Great Falls train near Glengarry, southwest of Lewistown. The steam locomotive, mail-express-baggage car, and coach are representative of hundreds of such short trains that daily plied the rails throughout North America during the first half of the twentieth century. As biographer Mary Clearman Blew wrote of her aunt, Imogene Welch, who traveled by train or bus from western Washington to Danvers, eighteen miles northwest of Lewistown, in May 1943: "The public transportation available to her in the 1940s is enviable." The Milwaukee ended its Harlowton–Great Falls passenger service in 1955.

family and national events at the NP passenger station. Marjorie Smith wrote:

> We old-timers and 'U-turners' remember coming and going there. We saw General Dwight D. Eisenhower campaigning on the back of a train in 1952. It's where I first saw my in-laws when they arrived from Boston a couple days before the wedding. Now there's a place teeming with memories.[11]

Recalling Montana's railway heyday, chapter 1 provides an overview of the technology and business of railroads and related consequences of standard time and settlement, with a summary of the rail network in Montana. Chapter 2 reviews the stations, trains, and the section crews that maintained the tracks. Chapter 3 covers the small-town combination passenger-freight stations, including the work and activities there. Chapter 4 features large urban terminals. Chapter 5 is about the trains and railway work in the right-of-way: what people along the tracks saw and what passengers saw from the car windows. Finally, chapter 6 covers the explanations and consequences of the diminishing, and even the disappearance, of railways in business and operations and in the lives of Montana's people and communities.

CHAPTER 1

Montana's Railway "Main Street"

RAILROADS reached Montana a half century after a revolution in land transportation, which began in England in the mid-1820s and reached eastern North America just a few years later. In the early 1940s, the Northern Pacific Railway (NP) adopted the corporate nickname "Main Street of the Northwest" in addition to its older moniker "Yellowstone Park Line." The new Main Street phrase was displayed on items ranging from paper timetables to the sides of streamlined diesel-electric locomotives. The nickname referred to the NP's transcontinental main line that linked the primary urban corridors of North Dakota, Montana (concentrated between Missoula and Billings), and Washington, including the capital cities of North Dakota and Montana. The NP was crucial in creating this corridor of transportation, settlement, and economic development between Minnesota and Puget Sound and published promotional materials describing itself as "First of the Northern Transcontinental Railroads." In 1950, Northern Pacific main lines served five of the six largest cities in Montana (excepting Great Falls) and six of the eight state-operated institutions of higher education, including two community colleges. Currently, over thirty-five years after the end of regular passenger rail service across southwestern Montana, the Missoula-Billings corridor is now commonly identified in terms of the highway next to the still active track of the former Northern Pacific: the I-90 corridor.[1]

Ron V. Nixon, photographer MOR RVN 14462

In decades past, railroads used the sides of boxcars to clearly display company identity in some combination of corporate name, nickname, motto, emblem, or name of its premier passenger train. This Northern Pacific boxcar standing next to a grain elevator in Bozeman on September 8, 1948, carries the railway's recently chosen "Main Street of the Northwest" motto and the East Asian monad emblem it adopted in the 1890s. Through the mid-twentieth century, boxcars with wooden interior doors carried grain from small country elevators to large terminal elevators and flour mills. During the 1970s, top-loading and bottom-dumping covered hopper cars replaced boxcars for this task.

The North American Railway Network

Railways were the world's first mechanically powered, all-weather land transportation. While some aspects of railroads—such as the size of locomotives, materials for bridges, and speed of trains—have changed greatly in nearly two centuries of operations, the characteristic elements of a railway have remained constant. From the 1820s, the railway has had three definitive components, two physical and one organizational. The first is the fixed property, centered on the distinctive feature of the track: two parallel iron or steel rails fastened to wooden crossties. The track rests on an earthen grade, interrupted at bridges and in tunnels. Close to the track, wires tied to glass insulators on the pole line carried telegraph and telephone traffic. Buildings, including stations, and other structures necessary for the operation of trains are also located within the right-of-way.

The second component is the "rolling stock" riding on the track: locomotives pulling cars designed for carrying either passengers or freight. Steam locomotives provided the power through the nineteenth century. During the twentieth century, they were partially supplanted by electric engines, then fully replaced by

Ron V. Nixon, photographer, MOR RVN 19703

The train order station of De Smet lay six miles west of Missoula at the junction of two main lines, the original one north to the Flathead River and a later route west along the Clark Fork River. The two routes rejoined at Paradise. The photograph, taken on July 6, 1955, shows the primary features of a main line railroad: multiple tracks connected by crossovers, the telegraph-telephone line with several cross-arms of insulators and wires, the small telegraph office with train-order signal rising above the roof, and a few of the buildings associated with the maintenance-of-way section crews based there. Most of the buildings for the section gang are out of sight beyond the station.

W. T. Cheney, photographer, MHS, PAc 80-17.58

Railway features are clear in this 1902 photograph of the Union Pacific's Pocatello-Butte main line south of Lima: the track on a low earthen subgrade, right-of-way wire fences on both sides of the track, and two pole lines. The snow-covered Lima Peaks of the Beaverhead Mountains dominate the skyline.

diesel-electric power. The rails supported trains and also guided the flanged wheels of the rolling stock. Because of their unprecedented capabilities, railways brought great change to commerce and travel everywhere, as well as radical alteration to conceptions of distance and time. One train—a locomotive pulling a long string of cars and operated by a crew of several workers—carried much larger loads at greater speeds than could be handled by dozens of drivers on animal-pulled wagons or coaches. Trips that previously required days, weeks, or even months could be accomplished, respectively, in hours, days, or, at most, a week—and at a lower cost with greater comfort for travelers.[2]

The third component is the private ownership of nearly all railways in the United States. By the mid-nineteenth century, governments incrementally intervened in railway operations. Growing public dissatisfaction over rail rates, schedules, facilities, and safety resulted in regulation of railway services and labor, at both state and federal levels. The Interstate Commerce Commission was the first federal agency to regulate business activity; it was established in 1887 specifically to oversee railroads. In Montana, the state legislature created the Board of Railroad Commissioners in February 1907. That agency, with broader duties, is now called the Montana Public Service Commission.[3] Government regulations included legal definitions of railways' obligations to the public. Railroads were designated "common carriers," required to accept public business for passengers, express, and freight. As Montana state law defined duties for freight: "A common carrier must, if able to do so, accept and carry whatever is offered to him, at a reasonable time and place, of a kind that he undertakes or is accustomed to carry." For passenger service, the state required published schedules of operations.[4]

Government also supported some railroads in their developmental stages. In the United States, beginning in the 1850s, some railroads in the Midwest and West received government subsidies during construction, primarily through large grants of public lands. The grants were intended to provide revenue to the railroads through sale of the lands to settlers, corporations, and speculators. In Montana, the only railroad to receive federal land grants was the Northern Pacific through its congressional charter enacted in 1864. In 1900, seventeen years after the Northern Pacific completed its main line across the state, the NP owned 20,736 square miles of granted land, approximately one-seventh of the state's total area.[5]

By the late 1800s, railroads in the United States were, according to historian Alfred Chandler, the "nation's first big business." More than a dozen major railway companies each had operations, properties, and employees located in hundreds of places across many states. To manage such dispersed activities, the companies had to develop standardized practices. According to Chandler, "The railroads were the first American business to work out the modern ways of finance, management, labor relations, competition, and government regulation." This trend occurred because "their capitalization, their plant and equipment, their running expenses and labor force were much larger than those of any other business of that day."[6] Further examples of railways' standard practices included civil and mechanical engineering, train scheduling and dispatching, communications, and many types of buildings and structures. For instance, while railway stations varied across the Midwest and West in some architectural and decorative aspects, they were reassuringly familiar to travelers everywhere for their similarities in functions, staffing, and interior arrangements.

One obvious aspect of the standardization of railway operations was the growing prevalence of "standard gauge" (four feet, eight and one-half inches between railheads) across almost all of

F. Jay Haynes, photographer, MHS, H-3802

This photograph of the Northern Pacific Railway general offices in St. Paul, taken on March 14, 1899, shows the building at Fourth and Broadway. Railways governed operations and properties from corporate general offices, with policies and directives conveyed through offices overseeing regional operations to division headquarters along the main lines. Halfway up the central portion of the nearer, older part of the building, the terra-cotta ornamentation includes the lettering "NORTHERN PACIFIC R. R. Co." just above a representation of a Native American head with a feathered headdress. The building's corners display small medallions with the interlaced letters "N" and "P." The sign for the Minneapolis & St. Louis Railroad passenger station directs people to the terminal from which trains to Iowa and eastern South Dakota departed.

Courtesy the author

The Railroad and Bank Building, completed in 1916 and shown in this postcard view, housed the general offices of the Great Northern and the Northern Pacific Railways, structurally separated inside the building, as well as the First National Bank of St. Paul, recently acquired by James J. Hill. While the two railroads competed between Minnesota and Puget Sound, the business syndicate headed by Hill controlled them both after the mid-1890s.

North America. At places where tracks of different gauges met, all passengers and freight had to transfer between the cars built to each gauge. The first rail line into Montana, linked to the Union Pacific portion of transcontinental line completed in 1869, began from northern Utah in 1871 with "narrow gauge" track—three feet between the rails—to reduce the costs of construction, equipment, and operations. The Union Pacific acquired the line in 1877 and completed it to Butte in 1881. To make it fit better within its own network and the larger national system, the UP converted it to standard gauge in July 1887.[7]

The greatest example of railroad standardization occurred shortly after railroads reached Montana. The railroads of the United States and Canada acted together to implement a better coordinated system for keeping time on a continental scale suited to a method of transport that required reliable connections in published schedules. Until November 1883, local time was set independently by determining "noon" at thousands of towns and cities when the sun reached its highest point in the sky. Each railroad needed to have

Photographer unknown, MHS, Lot 33 B4.F8.04

Two narrow-gauge locomotives descend southward after helping a train headed to Butte over Monida Pass on the Idaho-Montana border. The narrow gauge track belonged to the Utah & Northern, a Union Pacific subsidiary. Although narrow gauge railways usually cost less to build, the inconvenience of transfers with the country's standard gauge railroad network resulted in most being converted to wider track. The Union Pacific hired four hundred workers for just one day, July 24, 1887, to convert the 262 miles of track from Pocatello to Butte.

consistent time standards within their network based on "the local time of the most important or most central stations" and applied to all stations across their network. But companies did not coordinate among themselves. In the summer of 1883, several months before the implementation of universal standard time, Union Pacific trains into Butte from northern Utah ran on "Salt Lake time." Northern Pacific schedules in Montana on the nearly completed transcontinental line were based on "St. Paul time," behind either forty-five minutes or one full hour, respectively, east or west of Billings. On November 18, 1883, a little over two months after the ceremonial completion of the NP at Gold Creek, Montana, the railways in the United States and Canada replaced local times and their independent operating times with four standard time zones (five in Canada). All railways adopted the new time zones centered on regularly spaced meridians west of Greenwich, England.[8]

For over three decades, this time zone measure applied officially only to railroads and was not mandatory for governments, businesses, and individuals. There was much opposition initially, but the centrality of rail transportation and associated timekeeping led almost everyone to eventually accept the new system. This acceptance was accompanied by the public's increased concern for time accuracy. Throughout the nation's rail stations, railroaders, travelers, and townspeople could find "standard time" clocks regularly checked by telegraph for accuracy. One historian noted, "The general public, increasingly anxious about the accuracy of its timepieces, checked pocket watches and clocks against the time displayed on the station tower or, in most stations, on an inside wall."[9]

The implementation of standard time brought a new, and now familiar, feature to maps: boundaries of the time zones. These boundaries are currently defined in the United States by the borders of states and counties and are the result of decades of adjustments. Initially, time zone borders were set at towns where two railroad operating divisions—where trains changed crews and locomotives—met close to the appropriate meridian of longitude. When the federal government first recognized standard time zones and took control of setting the borders in 1918, it, too, combined considerations of meridians and towns that were railway operating bases. Almost all of Montana fell within the Mountain Standard Time zone, with the westernmost portion in Pacific Time. Through changes and adjustments in time zone borders in the twentieth century, two towns in northwestern Montana became part of the boundary between Mountain and Pacific time zones—Paradise on the Northern Pacific and Troy on the Great Northern. In timetables and travelers' guides, the change of time zone was noted. A Northern Pacific passengers' guide warned, in italics, in its text for Paradise: *"Note—westbound passengers should turn their watches back one hour here. Eastbound passengers should turn theirs one hour ahead."*[10] The Federal Writers' Project volume *Montana: A State Guide Book,* issued in 1939 and largely organized around auto tours of the state, noted that Troy and Paradise were significant as railroad division points where Mountain and Pacific Standard Times met.[11]

The economic and social impact of railways included their great demand for labor. Railroad companies were the largest and most dispersed employers in the United States. From remote telegraph stations and track maintenance bases to locomotive repair shops where thousands worked, railroads had employees in virtually every community they served as well as between widely spaced towns. Rail employment in the United States peaked around 1920, when two million people worked for the railways, an average of one out of every fifty Americans. (In 2018, the proportion of railroaders within the national population was less than one out of every two thousand.) Almost all railroaders were men, and the main area of railway work open to women was as telegraph operators. In the United States in 1920, only two census-defined economic sectors employed more people than railways: agriculture and retail businesses.[12]

In Montana, rail employment reached its apex in the mid-1910s as work was finished on lines completed during the previous half-decade. At that time, there were about twenty-three thousand rail workers in the state, including about two hundred women, or about one in every twenty-five Montana residents. Since then, Montana, with an unusual density of rail mileage, continues to have a greater proportion of railroaders in the population than nationwide. The number of railroad workers in 2018 was about one out of every four hundred Montana residents.[13]

Railroads also shaped human landscapes. In some parts of the world, in much of Europe, for example, railways were built in densely populated landscapes of towns and cities, thoroughly developed

Photographer unknown, MHS, Lot 35, B11/12.09

The Chicago, Burlington & Quincy main line from Nebraska to Billings, completed in 1894, crossed the Crow Indian Reservation in southeastern Montana. At the settlement and reservation headquarters of Crow Agency in July 1915, members of the Crow Nation stand between a Burlington train and an irrigation ditch.

Photographer unknown, UM, 76.0333

Horse-pulled vehicles await a passenger train at the Northern Pacific station for Stevensville, twenty-eight miles south of Missoula. The NP's Bitterroot branch line was built west of the Bitterroot River in 1887–88, bypassing the already existing town of Stevensville east of the river. Thus, the town's railway depot was across the river and over one mile from the town. The horse-pulled wagons shown at Stevensville station had probably delivered passengers, mail, and express and were ready to return to town after the train's arrival. Historical geographer James Shortridge wrote of the "particular two-tiered transportation system" that dominated the rural American landscape into the second decade of the twentieth century: "Railroads were one component, an efficient national network," and horses were the other, one that "implied a tremendously more restricted circle of activity."

with agriculture, industry, and transport on rivers and canals. In these areas, railroads brought obvious changes to transportation but narrowly limited alteration to the landscapes. In other parts of the world, however, railways reached across sparsely populated lands often far from navigable rivers. There, the rails often brought the first full exercise of power by a distant national government, including large military forces and political integration, which frequently included the subjugation or removal of indigenous peoples. One of the largest sparsely populated areas in the world that was shaped by railways was the central and western portion of North America. Rail lines were instrumental in transforming the human landscape—in particular, the location of new population centers, large-scale economic enterprises, government institutions, and, eventually, networks of highways.[14]

The railroad landscape of the late nineteenth and early twentieth centuries was shared with a much older technology—wagons and carriages pulled by horses. Trains and horse-drawn vehicles comprised "a particular two-tiered transportation system" described by geographer James R. Shortridge in his study of Junction City in eastern Kansas: "Railroads were one component, an efficient national network" that offered quick and low-cost travel over great distances for business, pleasure, and higher education. "The other primary means of transportation, the horse, counterbalanced this connectivity. Horses implied a tremendously more restricted circle of activity."[15] The distance horses and wagons could travel in a day, from farm to town and return, became a major consideration for farmers and agricultural researchers, especially in relation to access to grain elevators and other railway services. One historical geographer wrote, "If the [grain] elevator were no more than eight miles away, a farmer could make one round trip in a day, including loading, hauling, waiting, unloading, and returning to his farm."[16] Many towns and shipping facilities along rail lines in the Great Plains were established, in part, on such considerations.

Patterns of Railways in Montana

The development of a network of railways was essential to the level of economic activity achieved in Montana in the late nineteenth and early twentieth centuries for two reasons. First, Montana and its products were remote within the interior of North America, far

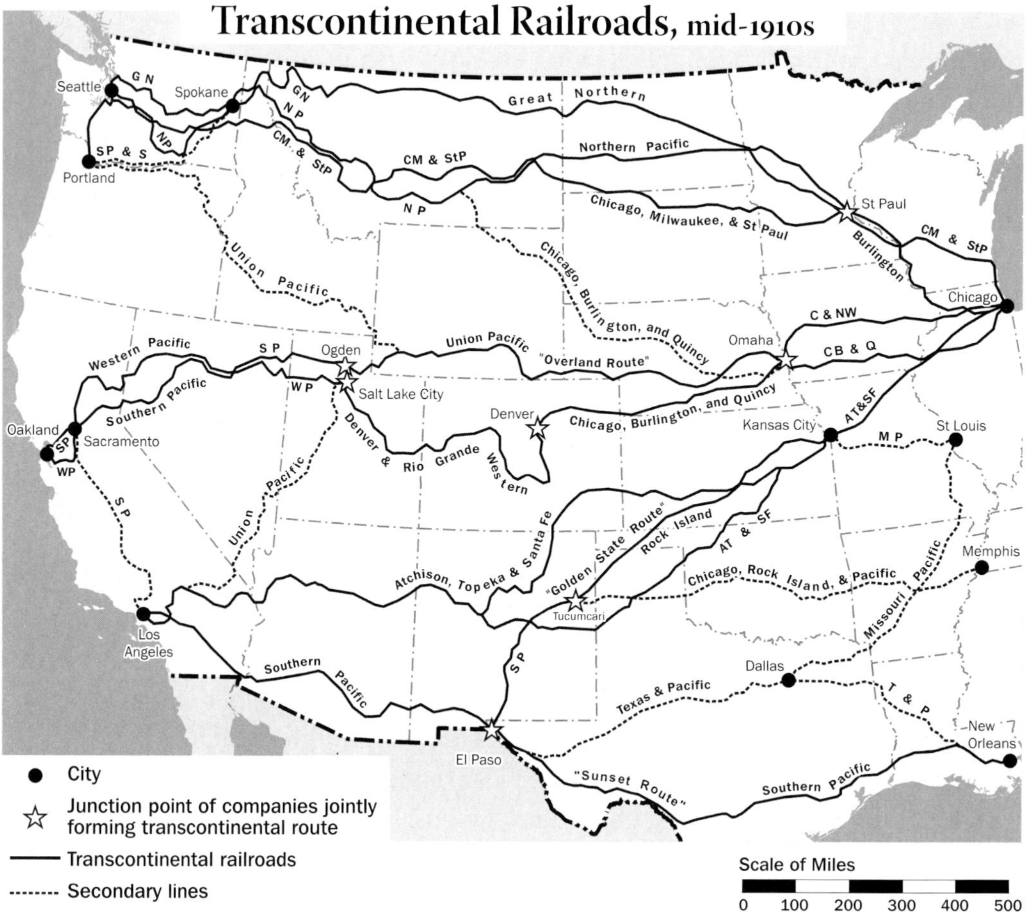

Map by Gerry Daumiller

from metropolitan markets and industry such as Minneapolis–St. Paul, Denver, Salt Lake City, and Seattle. Montana was also distant from the export potential of seaports and from the Mississippi and lower Missouri river ports that flourished into the twentieth century. Second, the economics of the state were then, and remain today, largely based on a combination of growing or extracting, processing, and shipping the bulky products of farms, ranches, forests, and mines, with most of those commodities intended for distant markets. Many of these goods—whether a ton of coal, a bushel of wheat, or a thousand board-feet of lumber—have a relatively low value per unit of weight or volume. Access to a very efficient, low-cost network of transportation was required for Montana commodity producers to earn a profit after delivery to faraway places. In 1918–19, the Montana commodities shipped in the largest quantities by rail, ranked by carloads, were metallic ores and concentrates (mostly copper, zinc, and lead-silver), coal for

Photographer unknown, MHS, Lot 35, B2/4.08

In the late nineteenth and early twentieth centuries, wool was one of Montana's major products. After shearing, the fleeces were packed into very large bags and transported to railroad-owned wool warehouses for shipment in boxcars to processing plants. In this Billings photograph, a line of wagons waits to unload.

commercial sale and railroad use, wheat and flour mill products, livestock (especially cattle and sheep), and lumber mill products.[17]

Almost all Montana's rail network developed between 1880 and 1920. Montana was the last of the forty-eight contiguous states and territories to be reached by a railroad.[18] In the forty years after the first rails reached Montana Territory in 1880, railways built 5,023 route miles of track, consisting of almost all single track with passing sidings.[19] Beside the tracks, companies established communities to serve as rail-operating and maintenance bases, including several large locomotive and car repair shops and hundreds of stations to serve the public and facilitate train movements. This network of tracks, trains, stations, and towns would flourish into the 1920s and, especially along main lines, endure into the 1960s.

As in most of the western United States and Canada, the rail system of Montana was oriented around east-west transcontinental main lines. In the American West, the term "transcontinental" describes a rail line, operated by one or more companies, linking a terminal city in mid-America with a port on the Pacific Coast. These lines generally divided into three corridors: the northern between St. Paul and Puget Sound, the central between Omaha and San Francisco Bay, and the southern from either Chicago, Kansas City, or New Orleans to Los Angeles.

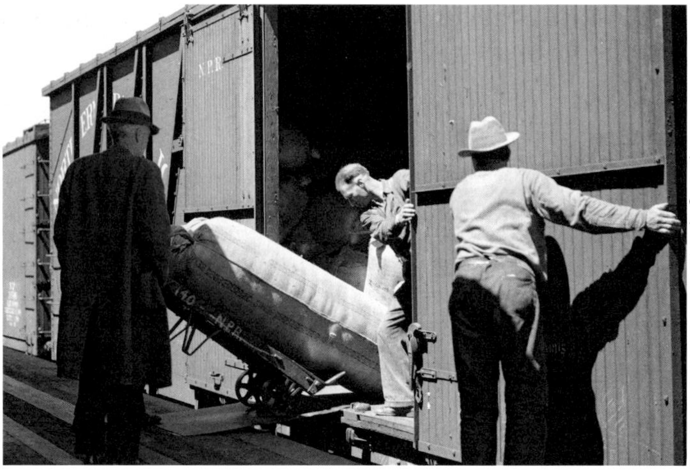

The presence of a photographer at the Northern Pacific's freight house in Livingston has attracted an ample crew to load large bags of wool from the Harvat ranch near town into a boxcar in 1937. The wool sacks held about forty fleeces, for a total weight of about three hundred pounds.

After 1909, the northern corridor had three transcontinental lines—one more than either the country's central or southern corridors. All three crossed Montana between the North Dakota border and the Idaho panhandle. The Northern Pacific completed its line across southern Montana in 1883. Ten years later, the Great Northern finished its main line across northern Montana to Seattle, and on the plains, it became the defining element of the corridor of towns and transportation commonly called the Hi-Line (originally spelled "High Line").[20] The Chicago, Milwaukee & St. Paul Railway, later popularly called the Milwaukee Road, finished its transcontinental route in 1909, with much of its line close to the Northern Pacific.[21] Because of its location between Minnesota and the ports of Puget Sound and its great east-west extent—nearly one-third of the distance between Chicago and Puget Sound—Montana had over 2,200 miles of transcontinental main lines for the seven decades from 1910 to 1980. Montana's transcontinental mileage resulted in a high density, in contrast to other western states, of well-engineered and heavily trafficked mains, division point operating bases, located at intervals of 100 to 150 miles, and unionized railroad employees.[22]

The three transcontinental lines added secondary and branch lines primarily to reach areas with major agricultural and mining activity. Two additional large western railroads operated secondary lines into the state: the Union Pacific from northern Utah and southern Idaho to Butte and the Chicago, Burlington & Quincy (Burlington Route) with two routes into Billings from the south and southeast.

The resulting network of east-west rail routes in Montana made travel in other directions more difficult. In central Montana, Great Northern secondary lines, centered on Great Falls, linked its transcontinental route to the Northern Pacific at Helena, Butte (the NP and the Milwaukee), and Billings. Even with these routes, rail travel between points in northern Montana and the more populous southwestern portion of the state was often complicated and inconvenient. Such a trip usually required riding several trains, often with long layovers at Havre or Shelby, Great Falls, or Helena. Historian Robert Athearn grew up in Havre and began college there in the early 1930s. He later recalled the role of travel in continuing his university education outside Montana:

> Here American geography and history intervened to shape a career. Since major western railroads run east and west, it was easier and possibly quicker to board Jim Hill's "Empire Builder," as the crack Great Northern train was called, and to head for Minneapolis than to work one's way down the ladder of roads to the state university in Missoula. The fact that Minnesota's out-of-state tuition was ten dollars per quarter higher than that charged the natives was a barrier that could be surmounted.[23]

Ron V. Nixon, photographer, MOR RVN 22814

A mechanical loader dumps sugar beets into high-sided open cars near Corvallis in the Bitterroot Valley on October 3, 1958. In 1928, the Northern Pacific relocated twenty-five miles of branch line from the west side of the Bitterroot River to the east side to better serve the irrigated beet fields.

There were also a variety of independent short lines and industrial operations in Montana. Local capitalists and investors built where larger railroads saw little reason to do so. The short lines, like the branches of larger railways, were usually built to link main lines to areas of farming, logging, or mining activity. Small-scale industrial railways worked inside smelters and sugar beet plants. Temporary lines were used into the 1930s to reach dams under construction.[24]

During the economic boom decade of the 1910s, Montana saw near completion of its network of rail lines, which were distributed throughout the state to a greater extent than lines in either neighboring Idaho or Wyoming. By 1920, tracks had reached nearly all well-settled parts of Montana, including forty-eight of the fifty-one counties. Of the 107 incorporated towns and cities reported in the 1920 U.S. census, only two, Ekalaka (population 433) and Virginia City (population 342), were not reached by rail. The largest unincorporated population centers without railways included Saint Ignatius in the Flathead Valley and Opheim (which was reached by rail in 1926) in the far northeast, each with a rural district population of over 1,000.[25] Within Montana, railways never reached the Rocky Mountains between Glacier National Park and the Helena-Marysville area, the southeast corner, and the "Big Open" in the center of eastern Montana. While the Great Northern planned a line across the Big Open in the mid-1910s and began earthwork east of Lewistown, it abandoned the project by the end of the decade.

Montana' s railways were exceptional in several ways. Through much of the mid-twentieth century, Montana had a greater concentration of railway mileage where electric power pulled heavy freight and passenger trains than any place outside the eastern United States. Electric rail lines were distinctive in appearance, with trains drawing power from an intricate array of cables and wires suspended above the tracks and substations located along the line. In 1913, the Butte, Anaconda & Pacific Railway pioneered electric power in the western United States for all railway functions of heavy freight, switching, and passenger service. Its success helped inspire another widely publicized example of electrification, that of the Milwaukee Road's main line from Harlowton in central Montana to Avery in northern Idaho, a distance of 440 miles. In the 1920s, this section and another 209 miles long in Washington comprised what the railroad advertised as "The World's Longest Electrified

Photographer unknown, MHS, PAc 2013-50.1159

This postcard photograph shows three railroads in the confines of Silver Bow Canyon at Durant, fourteen miles west of Butte. The photographer is standing next to the main line of the Butte, Anaconda & Pacific Railway, with poles supporting the overhead cables, insulators, and electric wires. A small crowd gathers near a loaded baggage truck in front of the Durant two-story train order station. The Northern Pacific main line is just to the right. At far right, a Milwaukee Road passenger train heads west under electric power.

Railroad—649 Miles of Transcontinental Line Now Operated by 'White Coal.'"[26] On a smaller scale, seven cities in Montana had electric street railways.[27]

In a configuration unusual in the West, railroads in Montana reached the borders of two national parks: Yellowstone and Glacier. Before automobile travel became common in the 1920s and 1930s, trains brought most of the visitors to these parks. The railroad companies supported legislation creating the parks and then promoted travel to them. Railways or their subsidiaries owned facilities and services for visitors, such as hotels and stage and bus transportation linking rail terminals with park lodgings.

Yellowstone, the country's first national park, is almost entirely within Wyoming, with only thin strips in Montana and Idaho.

Milwaukee Road photograph, MHS, PAc 80-63.8

A photographer working for the Milwaukee Road took this 1941 photograph of the *Olympian* passenger train approaching the switch for a passing siding in the Bitterroot Mountains. The complexity of electrification is evident in the cedar poles supporting the overhead array of cables and insulators required to suspend double trolley wires directly above the track and the crossarms carrying the wires for electrical supply and control. The locomotive's pantograph conducts the direct current from the trolley wires to motors inside the locomotive. Not shown in the photograph are two additional pole lines, one for telegraph-telephone lines and another carrying 100,000-volt power to the substations along the tracks.

However, during several early decades, most visitors reached the park by trains through towns in Montana, from the north and west. In 1883, eleven years after the park's creation, the Northern Pacific built the first rail line nearly to the park's border, at Cinnabar, Montana, the branch was extended three miles to Gardiner in 1903. The NP took the corporate motto "Yellowstone Park Line" and added those words to its corporate emblem—the red and black monad adapted from East Asia. On the west side of Yellowstone, the Union Pacific reached West Yellowstone from the south in 1908. Only with the rise of motor vehicles in the 1920s would significant numbers of visitors enter Yellowstone from Wyoming.[28]

In northwestern Montana, Glacier is the only national park with a rail main line and several stations along one edge. About twenty-three miles of the park's southern boundary is legally defined as the northern edge of the former Great Northern Railway (now BNSF Railway) right-of-way. In 1921, eleven years after creation of Glacier Park, the Great Northern adopted an emblem with the profile of a mountain goat.[29]

One hundred years ago, the people of Montana, either unaware of or indifferent to the railways' still-developing legacy, considered them an essential part of their life and work. The pervasiveness of railways was evident in two ways: first, the wide variety of transportation services available at most Montana towns and cities, and, second, the large number of populated places reached by passenger and freight trains.

The density of railway services available in 1920 is evident when comparing the number of places served by one particular passenger train with all the places in Montana now reached by public transportation. The 1920 Montana transportation options included a pair of local trains in northeastern Montana on the Great Northern Railway main line east of Havre. Trains 223 and 224 were examples of daytime "locals" that stopped at many places through which

Milwaukee Road photograph, MHS, PAc 80-63.4

The electrification of the Milwaukee Road main line over the Rocky and Bitterroot Mountains required fourteen large substations located at intervals averaging thirty-two miles. Machinery inside the large brick buildings transformed the 100,000-volt alternating current delivered by the Montana Power Company to 3,000-volt direct current conveyed on overhead trolley wires to locomotives. Each substation had three operators so that one was always on duty. Operators lived with their families next to their work in Craftsman-style residences, with privies in the back. Substation No. 12 (numbered westward from Harlowton) was on the eastern slope of the Bitterroots at Drexel. The two tracks by the buildings are spurs, and the main track and siding are on the lower hillside.

Ron V. Nixon, photographer, MOR RVN 10652

A special train carrying military veterans stands at the Northern Pacific's terminal at the northern gateway to Yellowstone National Park at Gardiner on June 17, 1940. The nearly circular balloon track makes it possible to turn the whole train. On the hill behind is the Gardiner business district and the ceremonial entry arch President Theodore Roosevelt formally dedicated in April 1903. The railroad area in the foreground is now the Gardiner High School football field and running track.

Ron V. Nixon, photographer, MOR RVN 10659

Two dedicated railroad photographers who were also Northern Pacific employees took many of the photos included in this book. Warren McGee worked as a brakeman and conductor out of Livingston over the span of nearly forty years. Here, McGee, in his passenger brakeman uniform, poses at the back end of a Yellowstone Park branch train, just arrived from Gardiner, on June 17, 1940. Ron Nixon snapped this photograph on the same day he took the previous one of the special NP train at Gardiner. Nixon began his fifty years with the Northern Pacific as a telegraph operator and became train dispatcher and wire chief (manager) of its telegraph relay office in Missoula.

transcontinental "limiteds" passed at full speed. During their twelve-hour run between Havre and Williston, North Dakota, a distance of 309 miles, the trains stopped at up to sixty-one places, of which fifty-six were in Montana. About half of these stops were "flag stops," made only if specifically requested by passengers. The trains stopped in places ranging in size from the incorporated town of Wolf Point, with 2,098 residents, to the unincorporated rural district of Madras, with a population of 64.[30] In 2018, representative of modern-day America, daily scheduled intercity trains, buses, and airplanes served only forty-two towns and cities in the entire state of Montana.[31]

CHAPTER 2

Stations and Trains

A CENTURY AGO in towns, men and boys frequently gathered for talk and social company in several kinds of businesses where they were not usually paying customers, such as a livery stable or blacksmith shop. And they also went to the railway station to watch their fellow townspeople beginning or finishing ordinary travels on trains serving nearby towns and cities.

Stations

In the mid-1940s, the journalist and commentator William Allen White recalled returning from Kansas City on a train to his home town of Emporia, Kansas, a half century earlier: "When I stepped off the train at Emporia it was into a considerable crowd of idlers who in that day came to the station to see the two plug trains [using different routes] come in from Kansas City."[1] In Emporia and thousands of other large towns like it, observers saw much activity. On the town side of the station, doors into the waiting and express rooms opened onto a street, perhaps called Railroad Avenue or Front Street. Horse-and-wagon teams delivered passengers or express from an office on Main Street. On the railway side of the station, the telegraph operator sat in a windowed bay with a view of the track in both directions, receiving updates on the train's arrival. Also in the station office, clerks sold tickets and checked baggage.

Photographer unknown, UM, 84.0006

Four young men—station "idlers"—at Arlee, Montana, in about 1908 assume a familiar pose for the time, sitting on or leaning against a baggage truck on the station platform. Arlee is north of Missoula on the Northern Pacific main line. In 1908–09, in the hour after 4:00 P.M., two trains were scheduled to stop, a good time to lounge at the depot on a warm, sunny day.

Photographer unknown, MHS, Pac 79-7.16

A large array of express and baggage is assembled on the platform of the Great Northern station at Shelby on October 20, 1925. On the baggage trucks sit many large crates and trunks, boxes tied up with cords, milk cans, and large canvas laundry hampers. Often overlooked among the functions of railway express was the transportation of laundry for both commercial and individual customers. The sign on the distant building identifies it as a lunch room. Shelby was a busy junction of the transcontinental main line and secondary lines south to Great Falls, Billings, and Butte and north to the Canadian border at Sweet Grass, Montana–Coutts, Alberta.

On the platform, composed of brick paving blocks in a herringbone pattern, were flatbed "trucks" with large, spoked wheels loaded with baggage, express, and, in grimy canvas bags, U.S. mail.

A longtime resident of Semans in central Saskatchewan remembered the Canadian National Railways main line trains that served the town during the 1930s and 1940s. The arrival of one particular daily train, eastbound from Saskatoon, brought townspeople to the depot. "In the nice weather many of the Semans town folk would stroll up [to the depot] to see 'The Local' come in, usually around 9:15 p.m. and at times, the station platform was quite crowded."[2]

Short-story writer and Nobel laureate Alice Munro (born 1931) grew up in Wingham in southern Ontario, north of the city of London. Wingham was linked to London by the Canadian National Railways, on track originally operated by the Grand Trunk Railway. The daily passenger train, and sometimes the rail line it rode, were informally called the "Butter and Eggs" since farmers used it to deliver those farm products to the urban market of London. The train also brought the city to the country. Munro recalled Wingham station in autobiographical fiction: "Here we got the evening daily paper. There were two London papers, the *Free Press* and the *'Tiser* (*Advertiser*). The *'Tiser* was Grit [aligned with the Liberal Party] and the *Free Press* was Tory [Conservative]." The arrival of the train was very memorable to a child.

> In the evening we went to the station, the old Grand Trunk, or the Butter and Eggs, as it was known in London. One could put an ear to the track and hear the rumble of the train, far away. Then a distant whistle, and the air became tense with anticipation. The whistles became closer and louder and finally the train burst into view. The earth shook, the heavens all but opened, and the huge monster slid screaming with tortured brakes to a stop . . .[3]

Chet Huntley, who with David Brinkley anchored the NBC Evening News from 1956 to 1970, spent part of his youth living in Montana towns along the Northern Pacific Railway, for which his father worked as a telegraph operator. Huntley was born in 1911 in the living quarters of the NP station at Cardwell, forty miles east of Butte. While Huntley was in high school in the late 1920s, his father worked in the NP station in Whitehall, thirty-three rail miles east of Butte.[4]

There, in Whitehall's station, Huntley became the link between national and local communities. In his autobiography, he recalled his first "broadcasting" experience, on a weekend when company telegraph traffic was slow:

> My first experience in "mass communication" came as the result of Dad's trade as a telegrapher. On the days of a World Series game, if it was Saturday or Sunday, Dad would write down the play-by-play reports as they came over the wire. A cluster of people would gather in the waiting room of the station, and I would bellow through the ticket window the play-by-play action of the game.[5]

Station Definitions, Types, and Names

To most people a century ago, a railway station was a building next to the tracks where the staff retailed and managed the company's transportation and communications services. In the railway rulebook, however, a "station" was defined as a "place designated on the time-table by name."[6] The timetable referenced is the employee timetable that strictly guided the work of all operating railroaders, not the public schedules available to travelers. Under this definition as a named place, a "station" could be a major urban terminal, a staffed depot building in a small town, or a passing siding or spur track—without buildings or employees—away from a town.

In popular usage in the United States, the terms "station" and "depot" are used interchangeably, and this volume does the same when it is obvious the subject is a staffed building. But careful railroad usage, as on architectural standard plans and station plat maps, preferred "depot" for the building while "station" remained applicable to the place. The official name "terminal" was sometimes applied to large urban stations, such as the Los Angeles Union Passenger Terminal and the Cincinnati Union Terminal, where many trains began and ended runs.

Stations varied in scale and range of functions depending on the population and economy of the community. The presence of a college, government institution, or popular tourist destination might earn a town a larger depot. Of all the railway stations, the best known and remembered, and probably the most preserved, were those buildings intended to visually stand out in urban settings. They were prominent for a combination of their size, roofline, architectural design, and ornamentation. The presence of a tall tower, often with four clock faces, emphasized a station's profile. In Montana, railroads built large stations in major cities, for example, at Great Falls (GN and Milwaukee); in towns with railroad operating headquarters, like Glendive (on the NP); in other large towns with separate passenger and freight stations, such as Miles City (on the NP) and Lewistown (on the GN); and in tourist gateways such as West Yellowstone (on the UP). Some depots combined multiple categories: the NP station in Livingston functioned as division headquarters, a major junction, and a tourist gateway to Yellowstone Park.

At a large, busy passenger station on a main line, operations continued around the clock. Telegraphers conveyed dispatchers' orders to trains. Passenger trains scheduled for convenient times at major terminals inevitably stopped at some intermediate towns in the late evening or very early morning. Emmett B. Moore attended Montana State College in Bozeman in the early 1920s, and in the 1970s he recalled the schedule of Northern Pacific passenger trains through that town: "I REMEMBER . . . Waiting up many a night in Bozeman to catch or meet a train (they all seemed to arrive between 2:00 and 4:00 a.m.)." Moore's son noted, "He took the night train to the east out of Bozeman many times."[7]

At the other end of the spectrum of size and activity was the small-town combination passenger-freight station on a branch line. A single worker, the agent, performed all the work. As branch line trains usually ran during the daytime, the station was closed each night. Most were wood-frame buildings based on standard plans issued by the offices of the railroads' chief engineers. These were utilitarian structures for which the railways' main priority was the economy of materials and construction. Distinctive appearance was not a concern.

However fondly railway stations may be recalled now, travelers a century ago often found unpleasant conditions, and some railroaders were aware of this. An editorial in a 1915 railway journal noted, "Waiting in a railroad station is irksome to most people of energy, to say the least, especially when trains are late." Common complaints included "improper heating or ventilation" and "insufficient light for reading, by day or by night, or deficient or obscure toilet facilities."[8]

As railways built new lines across thinly settled landscapes of the West with few named inhabited places, they needed a place-name for each siding, a track connected at both ends to the main track, where one train could get off the main line to allow another to pass by. Many sidings were without buildings, structures, or residents before the tracks reached the spot. Railways drew on the names of nearby geographical features; of places elsewhere in the United States and beyond, including places in the news; the names of railroad officials and other employees and their family members; and more. Names of Native American origin were rare.[9] In some cases, the place's original name was changed—either by the railroad or by local settlers—especially after significant settlement supplemented basic railroad functions. The railroad town of Havre developed after 1890 and shed its first, less appealing name of Bullhook Bottoms.

One distinctive feature of place-names occurs along the Hi-Line with its notably high proportion of town and station names that are easily recognized as foreign places. In standard practice, the Great Northern and its predecessor, the Manitoba Road, assigned most of these names at, or just after, the time of construction. On the plains of northern Montana, thirty-two familiar foreign names appeared in the early GN timetables, including Glasgow, Paisley (which there, as it is in Scotland, is just west of Glasgow), Cork, Malta, and Simla (the summer capital of British India at that time).

Foreign Names on the Great Northern Montana Hi-Line

As shown on 1920 timetables

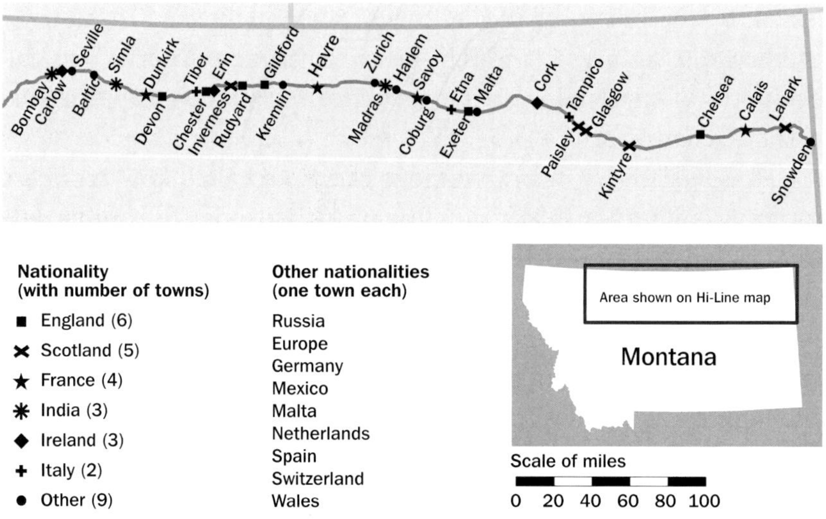

A commonly repeated story holds that a blindfolded employee in the railway headquarters stopped a spinning globe with a finger and the location he touched had its name placed on the railroad.[10] But the distribution of sources for the names conveys a more selective, though unknown, process. Nearly half the familiar foreign names from North Dakota to Washington were taken from Britain and Ireland. In Montana, Scottish and English place-names are noticeably prominent.

The railway's use of many familiar foreign place-names occurred in three separate phases. It began in 1886 as the Manitoba Road began building its "Montana extension" west from Devils Lake, Dakota Territory, and drawing almost all of its foreign place-names from English cities, such as Leeds, York, and Rugby. The following year, construction continued from Minot all the way to Great Falls. There was a greater variety of foreign sources for place-names west of Minot, with more from Britain but also from continental Europe and India, including Palermo, Calais, and Madras (for the city in India now named Chennai). The second phase was in 1890–93 as the renamed Great Northern built from Pacific Junction, just west of Havre, to Puget Sound and continued the diversity of overseas sources for names. Among these were Kremlin and Inverness in Montana, Naples in Idaho, and Odessa and Berne in Washington. The final phase was in 1910–12 when the GN built a new shortcut main line across eastern North Dakota. Here, German city names appeared, including Bremen and Hamburg, both major seaports through which many central Europeans emigrated to North America.

Train Order Stations

For one type of station, the primary purpose was their "necessity for proper and safe train movements, and not for the conduct of the carrier's commercial affairs."[11] One of the main tasks of operating trains on a busy single-track line was arranging "meets" between trains at passing sidings five to ten miles apart. While this mostly applied to trains going in opposite directions, it was also necessary for faster trains to be able to overtake slower ones going in the same direction. The primary guidelines for train movements were the employee timetable and the rule book, which set the priority of trains by passenger or freight and by direction. When the operation of one or more trains required alterations to these documents, a dispatcher at a division headquarters wrote "train orders"—with very specific directions to train crews—that were sent on wires on the trackside pole line to stations ahead of the trains, to be delivered to the trains' crews. By the 1910s, sending of train orders by telephone had replaced telegraphic transmission along many main lines. While the use of telephones allowed employment of operators not trained in Morse code, it also required more wires, with complicated positioning on crossarms on the pole lines. Thus, telegraph transmission of train orders and other railroad business remained in use along some main lines and most branch lines through the mid-twentieth century.

Where towns and smaller communities were common, as in much of the eastern United States, the delivery of train orders occurred at stations located at these populated places. Where settlement was sparse and towns far apart, as in Montana and much of the West, railroads established telegraph "train order" stations away from towns.

The delivery of orders to the train crews was the responsibility of operators in staffed depots. The operator copied the orders, with carbon-paper copies, and set the station signal ("order board" or

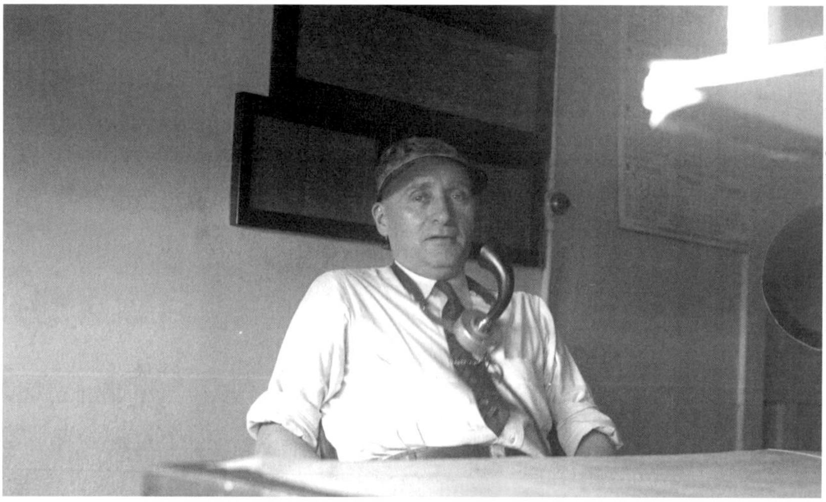

Ron V. Nixon, photographer, MOR RVN 01518

When operations varied from those detailed in employee timetables and the book of operating rules, a train dispatcher in a division headquarters wrote the orders to pertinent trains. The orders were sent by telephone or telegraph to operators in stations ahead of the trains for delivery to the crews. On an upper floor of the Northern Pacific station at Missoula, in October 1935, dispatcher Jimmy Jones works at his desk with a large sheet of paper on which to record train movements sent in by operators in stations along the line. A hands-free telephone mouthpiece for sending orders is suspended from a strap around his neck.

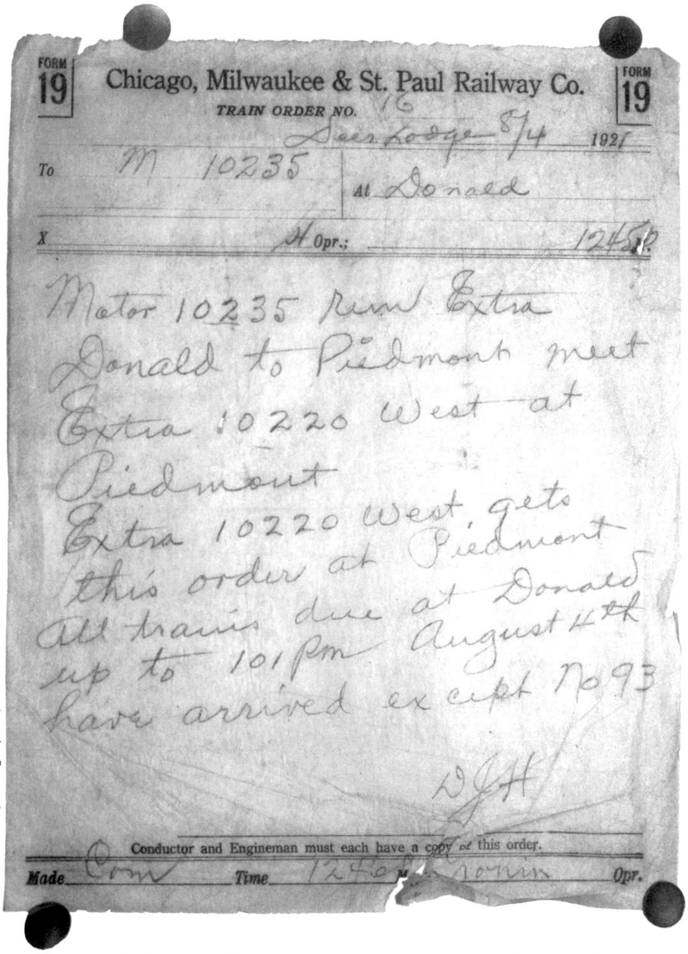

FORM 19 Chicago, Milwaukee & St. Paul Railway Co. FORM 19

TRAIN ORDER NO. 16

Deer Lodge 8/4 1921

To M 10235 At Donald

X H Opr.: 1245 P

Motor 10235 run Extra
Donald to Piedmont meet
Extra 10220 West at
Piedmont
Extra 10220 West gets
this order at Piedmont
All trains due at Donald
up to 101 pm August 4th
have arrived except No 93

DJH

Conductor and Engineman must each have a copy of this order.

Made Com Time 1246 P Opr.

Ron V. Nixon, photographer, MOR RVN 32784

This train order details operations on the Milwaukee Road's main line over the Continental Divide east of Butte on August 4, 1921. The train dispatcher at Deer Lodge sent the order to the operator at Donald, just east of the Pipestone Pass tunnel under the Continental Divide. The operator copied the order and delivered the Form 19 to the crew of electric freight locomotive Motor 10235 as it rolled by the depot. The order directed the movement eastward, its meeting with a westbound extra freight at Piedmont (twenty-one miles east of Donald), and noted that scheduled westbound freight No. 93 had not yet passed Donald.

just "board"), which was visible on a tall mast rising above the roof to indicate to the crew of the approaching train that it had orders to pick up. The crew on the locomotive received one set of orders. Another set of the same orders went to the crew in the caboose of a freight train or in the cars of a passenger train. This transfer could be accomplished when the train stopped and the crew came into the station, or the orders could be delivered while the train passed the station without stopping. As an operator who worked at the beginning of the twentieth century recalled:

> In delivering such an order, an operator stands alongside the tracks and holds up copies attached to long-handled hoops. The board being red, the engineer slows down and, as the engine slides past, the fireman or head brakeman leans from the gangway and, sticking out an arm, hooks the hoop with the engineer's copy as he passes, while the conductor or rear brakeman, from the caboose steps, scoops up the conductor's copy as the rear of the train rolls by the operator.[12]

The crews kept the orders and discarded the delivery hoop. Later, the crew took only the train order and the string suspending it in a quick-release fork, retained by the operator.

Perhaps the densest array of train order stations in Montana was along a short section of a heavy industrial rail line. The main line of the Butte, Anaconda & Pacific Railway connected the copper and zinc mines of Butte with the smelter at Anaconda. In 1916, with traffic of up to twenty freight and passenger trains in Montana per day, it was probably the busiest section of railway. All this traffic required closely spaced telegraph stations along the line. In the twenty miles between the large switchyards near each end of the main line, at Rocker and East Anaconda, the line had three telegraph stations with an average distance between them of five miles.[13]

Train order stations located away from towns were smaller than almost all other stations. There was no need for room for waiting passengers, baggage, express, or freight. Many began as the most basic "carbody" station—a retired boxcar lifted off its undercarriage (wheels, couplers, and brake gear) and set on a wooden footing next to the main track. The carbody was then modified with windows and interior details for use as a workplace and perhaps a residence. Many carbody stations were eventually replaced with small permanent buildings that included an office and living quarters for the operators. The Northern Pacific standard plan for an eighteen-by-twenty-four-foot "telegraph office with living rooms" included two bedrooms and a living room–kitchen. Stations of this plan were located at each end of the NP's tunnel under Bozeman Pass: Muir at the east end (with a rear extension on the office) and West End on the other side.[14]

Into the early twentieth century, a train order station that was operated around the clock had two operators, each working a twelve-hour shift. These hours changed in 1907 with the federal Hours of Service Act that, among many provisions, limited the hours for telegraph operators in twenty-four-hour stations to nine hours of work.[15] Railways either had to close the station part of each day or hire a third operator to keep a station open all day and night.

Remote train order stations were often located in small railway communities that also included track maintenance "section crew" housing and sheds and water facilities for filling locomotive tenders. Such trackside bases were one more example in the West's wide landscape of isolation and loneliness, much like remote farms and ranches or small mining camps. In his novel *Stepsons of Light,* Eugene Manlove Rhodes portrayed a character on horseback approaching a remote cluster of buildings on the Santa Fe Railway in south-central New Mexico: "Six miles brought him to Upham—side track, section house, low station, windmill tower and tank; there was a deep well here."[16]

There was an era of popular railway fiction from the late nineteenth century through the first half of the twentieth century that assumed readers' familiarity with railroading. Many stories featured telegraph operators at remote train order stations. The telegraphers, living in their small workplace, had only the company

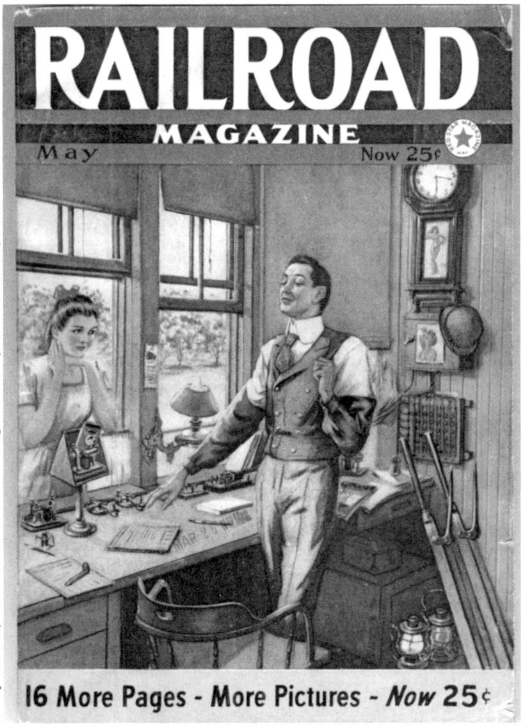

Harry C. Temple, illustrator, *Railroad Magazine*, May 1942. Courtesy White River Productions

This idealized and whimsical portrait on the cover of the May 1942 issue of *Railroad Magazine* shows the telegraph operator in a rural station. Inside the windowed bay are the telegrapher's tools: telegraph keys and receiving "sounders," one of which is in a wooden box with a Prince Albert can to amplify the clicks. There are also electrical circuit boards, train order forms, lanterns, and the large levers to set the train order signal, which is on a tall mast above the station roof, to alert approaching trains if there are train orders to receive.

of the track maintenance crew, which often consisted of recent immigrants with limited knowledge of the English language. On duty, especially at night, the lone telegrapher in a small station in a desert or mountain location was in a setting suitable for drama and psychological tension. "The typical isolated station lacked electric lighting, for example, and the operator sitting next to his kerosene lamp might well be surrounded by shadows. Indeed bad lighting lies at the heart of many ghost stories in railroad folklore and fiction."[17]

Ron V. Nixon, photographer, MOR RVN 26823

This May 1963 image shows train orders hooped up to a Burlington excursion train at the Northern Pacific station at Fromberg, thirty-eight miles southwest of Billings. The NP shared the track through Fromberg with the Burlington Route main line to Denver. Although the era of regular steam locomotive operations had ended, this passenger special featured steam engine 4960 with the assistance of a diesel-electric just behind it.

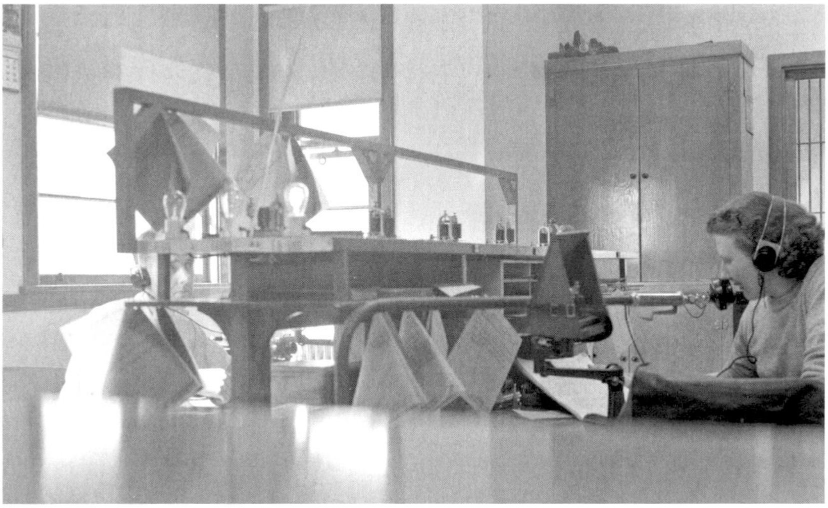

Ron V. Nixon, photographer, MOR RVN 08722

The reality of the telegraph operator's job was prosaic. Here, operator Rosie Presker speaks into a telephone mouthpiece while sitting behind the operator's bay in the Northern Pacific's new station at Paradise on October 13, 1944. Paradise is northwest of Missoula and was then both a junction of two main lines to the east and a crew change point. Also visible is a wooden box with a sounder, electrical gear, and suspended train orders and other papers.

Ron V. Nixon, photographer, MOR RVN 00974

Al Frazier, the operator at the Northern Pacific passenger station in Bozeman, hands up orders on a snowless December day in 1934. The engineer of the first locomotive, a helper assisting the train's larger road engine just behind it, is reaching out to grab the orders. The steep grade up to Bozeman Pass lies ahead. This train is an eastbound extra with refrigerator cars behind the power.

Stations on the Union Pacific

The variety of rail stations displaying the range of building sizes, functions, and community settings was well represented on the Union Pacific in Montana during the 1920s. The main UP property in Montana was the northern portion of a secondary main line from Pocatello, Idaho, to Butte, Montana—132 miles of main track from Monida Pass on the Idaho border to Silver Bow junction. The Union Pacific used track shared with the Northern Pacific for the final six miles east into Butte. The UP daily schedule included six trains, or three in each direction: two pairs of passenger trains and one of freight. Another Union Pacific line reached the national park entry town of West Yellowstone, to which the railroad offered seasonal service. There, the UP built a large one-story building of stone that included the usual station functions as well as dressing rooms where travelers could change between clothes for rail travel and for stage or bus travel inside the park. The Union Pacific oversaw its operations in Montana from the second and third stories of the building in Pocatello that housed the passenger station and regional administrative offices. At the other end of the main line, in Butte, the UP shared a two-story station at the base of the hill with the Northern Pacific.

Chris Schlechten, photographer, MOR x 80.6.1955

The Union Pacific carried many passengers from California and the Southwest to Yellowstone National Park through West Yellowstone, Montana, at the end of its branch line from Idaho Falls. The UP station, pictured here in 1940, housed facilities for passengers to change between clothing for the train and riding vehicles within the park, as well as showers for those leaving the park.

In 1923, the UP had eleven staffed stations along the line from Monida Pass to Silver Bow junction.[18] The largest town south of Butte was Dillon, with a 1920 population of 2,701. It was the seat of Beaverhead County and the location of Montana's first Normal School. Here, the UP had separate buildings for passenger and freight services. The brick passenger depot included a full second story in the central part of the building. Elsewhere along the line, the stations were wood-frame buildings that housed passenger and freight services, as well as telegraphers delivering train orders, and were often located next to track maintenance bases, water tanks, and railroad-owned stockyards. In the small town of Melrose, laid out with platted streets and blocks, all station functions were housed in a building twenty-four by seventy feet. Other stations were located in rural districts away from formal settlements and served as shipping points for livestock from stockyards. One example was Monida, at the crest of the pass with the same name on the state line. With an elevation of 6,820 feet, it was the highest pass crossed by a rail main line in Montana. The station there was a large building, twenty-four by ninety-five feet, with telegraphers on duty day and night.

Sometimes the railroad moved small buildings to meet changing business conditions and state regulatory rulings. This type of relocation happened at Apex, twelve miles north of Dillon, and Glen, seven miles north of Apex. Just a year or two after the UP built a sixteen-by-forty-foot depot at Apex in 1911, it moved the building to Glen to replace a small, unstaffed passenger shelter considered inadequate for the community's needs. That shelter was, in turn, moved south to Apex as a smaller substitute for the removed station building.

One remote station on the UP provided a Montana politician with a distinctive campaign nickname. The station was at Bond, six miles north of Dillon, where a daytime operator worked in a carbody depot. Burton K. Wheeler campaigned for governor in 1920 as a Democrat with the additional endorsement of the Nonpartisan League (NPL). The NPL support ignited strong opposition from those who considered it a radical and even dangerous organization. When the mood at a campaign rally on a ranch close to Dillon turned ominous, Wheeler quickly left. To avoid likely danger in Dillon, a ranch hand who was a Great War veteran drove Wheeler north to the depot at Bond. The driver went off to acquire a rifle and then returned and stayed with Wheeler. As Wheeler recalled in his autobiography, the intent was that he "would be able to catch a train for Butte that night. The railroad station turned out to be a boxcar parked on a siding, since the station served only as a loading point for cattle. There was no town within driving distance and only one farmhouse nearby." After angry opponents in automobiles arrived at the boxcar station, Wheeler's companion threatened to shoot anyone who got too close. The men continued the siege of the station and prevented Wheeler from boarding the night train. Eventually, the Silver Bow County sheriff arrived and drove Wheeler back to Butte. Wheeler wrote, "The episode prompted the opposition press to start referring to me as 'Boxcar Burt.'"[19] Wheeler lost the election for governor, but two years later he was elected U.S. senator and served in the Senate from 1923 to 1947. The story became a favorite of Wheeler's, retold many times.[20]

Passenger Trains

For many decades, Americans' primary knowledge of railroads was through passenger trains. These were the trains they rode, the trains that brought visiting family and friends, and the trains they saw frequently, either in their towns or crossing the landscape. In the early twentieth century, trains ranged from widely advertised expresses with famous names to unnamed two- and three-car local trains that slowly moved across the land, stopping every five to ten miles. The former are well remembered, the latter are not.

Some of the best-known passenger trains of the twentieth century operated on the transcontinental run between Chicago or St. Paul and Seattle or Tacoma. These trains offered the full range of services found on most premier trains. By the early twentieth century, there was a standard arrangement of cars and on-board services on most long-distance trains on overnight runs. Just behind the steam locomotive were the head-end cars carrying mail, express, and baggage, then coaches, next a dining car with a very compact kitchen preparing full meals, followed by sleeping cars with a range of accommodations, including curtained berths and compartment rooms. Usually, at the end was a parlor observation car with an open platform and brass railing. On the railing was a sign with either the train name or railroad emblem.

The premier named train of each railroad was integral to the

For most of the two hundred miles between Missoula and the headwaters of the Missouri River, main line passenger trains of the Northern Pacific and the Milwaukee Road operated within sight of each other. About twenty-five miles east of Missoula, in the late afternoon of April 14, 1941, Ron Nixon caught two trains that competed in the Puget Sound to Chicago corridor—Milwaukee's electric-powered *Olympian* (left) and NP's steam-pulled *North Coast Limited* racing eastward.

Ron V. Nixon, photographer, MOR RVN 11129

company's identity. The Northern Pacific ran its *North Coast Limited* for seventy years through Montana's southern urban corridor. From 1905 until 1929, the Great Northern *Oriental Limited* commemorated the railway's link to East Asian commerce. After 1929, it was supplanted by the *Empire Builder* that honored company founder James J. Hill. The Milwaukee Road ran the *Olympian,* with cars painted orange and maroon, unusual when most trains were dark Pullman green.

Many would assert that the high era of train travel was in the two decades after the Second World War, when multicolored, streamlined, diesel-powered, air-conditioned, sealed-window trains dominated the main lines. By the mid-1950s, many of these trains west of Chicago, including the premier trains on all three transcontinental lines across Montana, featured "dome cars" with metal-framed, many-faceted glass domes rising above the roofline of the train. Great Northern's *Empire Builder* across Montana had more seats under domes than any other train in North America. One historian described this post-1945 version of long-distance trains:

Ron V. Nixon, photographer, MOR RVN 11549

Most travelers fail to appreciate the passenger train for the miracle it is. In essence it forms a small city on wheels, with lighting, heating, air conditioning, food services, toilets, washrooms, a water supply, and sleeping, seating, and lounging facilities. . . . All these systems must be fitted into the cramped spaces available between the side panels, under the floor, and in utility closets. Space is at a premium, making miniaturization a necessity. Dependability, weight, and cost are also crucial factors. Perhaps even more remarkable, this 1,400-ton city on wheels crosses the countryside at 80 miles an hour through all extremes of weather.[21]

The first streamlined trains through Montana began operation in 1947, with significantly faster schedules than their predecessors pulled by steam locomotives. That year, Great Northern introduced the new *Empire Builder* train sets, and the Milwaukee reequipped the *Olympian* as the streamlined *Olympian Hiawatha.* The Northern Pacific's *North Coast Limited,* with a slower schedule burdened with stops at more cities and towns, was not sped up and fully reequipped until 1952.

In the decade after 1945, the railways extensively promoted the

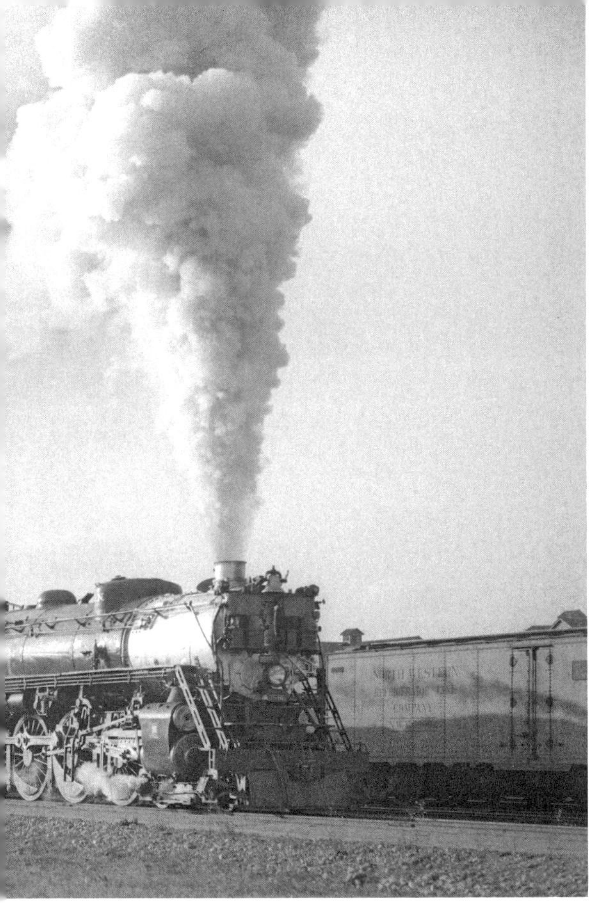

The Great Northern's premier transcontinental passenger train, the *Empire Builder*, departs eastbound from the division point of Whitefish on October 27, 1941. In the next sixty-nine miles, the locomotive will pull the train from an elevation of 3,040 feet to 5,215 feet at Marias Pass on the Continental Divide.

(following pages) The mountains that rise up to two-thirds of a mile above the former Great Northern main line on the southeastern boundary of Glacier National Park have long provided photographers with a dramatic backdrop. In this company photo, the *Empire Builder* of the 1950s and 1960s—diesel-powered and streamlined with dome cars—leaves the forested slopes for its eight-hundred-mile run across the Great Plains. Under the three glass domes near the front of the train and the car-length dome farther back are 147 seats for passengers in coaches and sleeping cars.

Great Northern Railway photograph, MHS, Lot 33 B2/10.04

new streamliners and "domeliners." Their publicity emphasized the contrast between streamliners and steam-locomotive-powered trains with only partial air-conditioning, where smoke and cinders came in open windows on hot days. The first appearance of a streamliner on a route—either on a publicity tour or beginning scheduled service—drew people to the tracks. Guy Clark grew up in west Texas and in his song "Texas 1947" conveys the novelty of first seeing the new, fast, and clean trains. He sings of the dozens of people who drove to the depot just to see the first run of the "fast-rolling streamline . . . screamin' straight through Texas." Clark finishes the song with people in their cars pondering the abruptness of change, and he recovers the nickel he had laid on top of a rail, now thinner than a dime.

Through the first half of the twentieth century, railroads competed fiercely for business on these trains, promoting them with a combination of fast schedules, material comforts, and amenities, such as a barbershop or library on board, and special menu items in the dining car (the NP featured its "Big Baked Potato"). The best-known trains also appeared in the news, especially when public figures rode them. The railroads had famous persons photographed

GREAT NORTHERN
GREAT NORTHERN

352C
352-C
REAT NORTHERN
GREAT NORTHERN RAILWAY

on, or by, the observation car platform with the drumhead sign displaying the name of either the train or company.

Railroads commissioned art to promote their trains, services, and destinations. The companies hired artists to portray their trains in the landscapes through which they passed. The scenes included national parks, the great hotels in the parks (some built and owned by railways), and other scenery of mountains, canyons, coasts, and terminal cities. Some railroads included images of the Native Americans whose lands the main lines crossed. The Great Northern, for example, featured portraits of individuals of the Blackfeet Nation of northwestern Montana. Railroads reproduced the art on large colorful posters that "were easily displayed in depots and ticket offices, in numbers far greater than was ever possible with original paintings."[22] The images also appeared on pamphlets, brochures, guidebooks, timetable covers, menus, postcards, and playing cards. Railroads also used art on posters and promotional publications to encourage agricultural settlement along their tracks, especially by homesteaders on public lands.[23]

The premier trains remain favorite topics of books and photo coverage—and a focus of nostalgia for past, and presumably better, times. Twentieth-century long-distance passenger trains are fondly remembered both for the luxury enjoyed by a few in the 1910s and 1920s and for the comforts available to most people traveling on midcentury air-conditioned, streamlined versions. The nostalgia for the latter is heightened by their relatively short existence—through the 1950s into the 1960s—a time when the railroads operated streamliners with corporate priority and active promotion. Premier passenger trains were especially expensive to operate, with large on-board crews—especially in the dining, lounge, and sleeping cars—and support facilities at terminals and along their routes. By the late 1950s, many railroads, unable to overlook the significant financial burdens of offering full passenger services, began to reduce advertising and promotion, downgrade equipment and on-board amenities, and even seek government permission to end operation of some trains.

Before 1945, most people in Montana and across North America did not regularly ride the named expresses. Instead, they rode slower secondary long-distance trains, with fewer amenities, or local trains running on branch lines and on portions of main lines. The latter included the "mixed train," essentially a freight

Photographer unknown, MHS, (bottom) 946-139 and (top) H-4715

Ticket offices and depots commonly featured artwork and photographs promoting the sights and scenery on western rail routes. St. Paul, Minnesota's Northern Pacific ticket office (top, circa 1895) touted its "Yellowstone Park Route to Montana and North Pacific Coast Points" on the corner of its building. The lower image of the NP's uptown office in Butte, Montana, shown circa 1904, displayed art and photos commissioned by the railroad to encourage travel on its lines. Among the items on the walls are framed artworks portraying trains and scenes along the NP route as well as farther destinations like Alaska.

...like to be "looked after" when you travel?
UNION PACIFIC RAILROAD
SERVING YOU AND YOURS...
is the pleasant duty of the 35 highly trained employees comprising the personnel on Union Pacific Domeliners.
They look after your comfort and safety...prepare taste-appealing meals for your enjoyment. Your wish is their command and we're proud of the way they reflect true western hospitality.
On your next trip to or from the West enjoy the finest in accommodations and service on a Union Pacific Domeliner—or Streamliner. There is no extra fare.
UNION PACIFIC
Railroad
Omaha 2, Nebr.
Dependable Freight & Passenger Service

Back cover of *Trains* magazine, October 1960, author's collection

This 1960 Union Pacific magazine advertisement conveys two messages—one intended and the other unintended. While touting the many employees available to provide a variety of services on the railroad's premier long-distance main line trains, it also reveals the high labor cost of operating such services. The front six men are the train and engine crew, who changed at intervals of approximately one hundred to two hundred miles: the conductor, engineer, fireman, and three brakemen. Behind them are twenty-eight workers who stayed on the train for the entire trip, serving in the dome dining car, sleeping cars, coaches, coffee shop–lounge for coach passengers, and dome lounge for sleeping car passengers.

The White Sulphur Springs & Yellowstone Park Railroad operated a twenty-three-mile short line between White Sulphur Springs and Ringling on the Milwaukee Road main line. To reduce the cost of providing passenger and express service, the railroad replaced the steam engine and passenger cars with a self-propelled railcar made by the same company that built Mack trucks. It is pictured at St. Charles, eight miles north of Ringling, on October 2, 1940. The rocking gait of the railcar on rough track and flat-tone air horn inspired the nickname "galloping goose."

Ron V. Nixon, photographer, MOR RVN 10830

train with one or two passenger cars. Internal combustion engines made possible the self-propelled railcar, or, as it often appeared in timetables, the "Motor." With a rolling gait on branch line track and a flat-tone air horn, local people often nicknamed it a "galloping goose." One of these ran on the White Sulphur Springs & Yellowstone Park short line between Ringling and White Sulphur Springs.[24] Many of the people who rode these trains were as often dissatisfied with their travel experience as people today riding on airplanes and intercity buses.

John H. White, author of a history of rail passenger cars, wrote:

> The existing books [on passenger trains and cars] concentrate on name trains and luxury cars, detailing the joys and splendors of first-class travel. It is easy for a reader to forget that the majority of passengers occupied coach seats, ate box lunches, and sat up all night. The more nostalgic literature deals in velvet-smooth rides with sunset vistas of mountain lakes through picture windows. There is no mention of the incessant rattle and clatter, or of the dust and cinders in pre-air-conditioned days. In fact travel by any mode, even by rail, is often a miserable experience.[25]

Photographer unknown, MHS, PAc 97-93.14157

One of the earliest successful self-propelled railcars relying on internal combustion power, the McKeen car—shown here on the Montana, Wyoming & Southern Railroad—was named for its inventor and manufacturer, William McKeen. He based his design on a type of small, fast naval vessel that appeared in the news at the turn of the twentieth century, the torpedo boat. The resulting car, with its sharp prow and porthole-like windows, became one of the most distinctive vehicles on railways in the subsequent decades. The Montana, Wyoming & Southern—a short-line coal carrier southwest of Billings—operated this McKeen car, purchased secondhand from a line in Iowa, from 1917 to 1933. Locals called it the "submarine" or "galloping goose." It could also serve as a locomotive, pulling a few cars, such as the baggage car and boxcars in this 1920 photo.

Examples of passenger trains and stations that annoyed and even angered Montanans appear frequently in the published annual reports of the state Board of Railroad Commissioners during the 1910s. Complaints concerning stations included buildings (and carbody stations) that were cramped, dirty, needed repair, or lacked a full-time agent. Train times were also topics of great discontent, with either poor connections at junctions or schedules that made it impossible to make short round-trips to a county seat or nearby market town within one day. Many people believed that where a railway did not have competition in a town or on a particular route, it made little effort to offer reliable, convenient, and comfortable services.

An example from northeastern Montana conveys the frustration felt in many rural areas. In 1917, the board investigated service on a Great Northern daytime train serving the branch line from the junction community of Bainville—on the main line thirty-eight miles west of Williston, North Dakota—through Plentywood to the end of track at Scobey. The branch was ninety-eight miles long, and the train was scheduled to take four hours. Citizens in Sheridan County complained about old and dirty coaches, overcrowding, and late trains.

The commissioners' report stated, "The complainants alleged that the passenger trains consisted of a combination mail and baggage car, and two small antiquated coaches, one of which was used as a smoker [where men smoked], and the other as a day coach, both of which were habitually kept in a foul, dirty, and unsanitary condition." Furthermore, the commissioners wrote, "The schedule on this line apparently means but little, and during the past winter in reality has been night service instead of day service." At the time the commission held hearings in Plentywood and Scobey,

> there were two coaches on this train, which although very old, had evidently been recently in the [repair] shops. The coaches were at that time equipped with steam heat, and were fairly clean and comfortable, although no spittoons [for tobacco chewers] were provided. It was evident, however, that there was not sufficient seating capacity afforded to accommodate all of the passengers. . . . [P]assengers were standing until arrival at Redstone [three-quarters of the way through the scheduled four-hour run].

Photographer unknown, MHS, PAc 2013-50.1236

A Great Northern branch line passenger train waits at Scobey in an era when both horse-pulled flatbed wagons and automobiles gathered at train time. The train is headed east to Bainville, the junction with the transcontinental main line. In March 1917, the state's Board of Railroad Commissioners traveled to Scobey, by train, to hear numerous complaints about the poor quality of passenger service and equipment on this line.

The commissioners ordered the Great Northern to improve service, including running cars with sufficient seating, cleaning the cars more frequently, and providing adequate heat and lighting.[26]

"Head End" Traffic

Much of the income railroads earned from passenger trains was from the cars at the front of the train, just behind the locomotive and ahead of the cars carrying passengers. These "head-end" cars carried goods requiring passenger-train speeds and the security of priority shipping: express parcels, money, U.S. mail, baggage, perishable foodstuffs such as cream and milk in steel cans, coffins, and even laundry shipped out of town for cleaning. All these could be seen on the flatbeds of the spoke-wheeled baggage trucks on station platforms just before train time.

Express service is defined as "the prompt and safe movement of parcels, money, and goods at rates higher than standard freight rates." Express companies were either independent firms, such as Wells Fargo, or subsidiaries of railroads, such as the Northern Pacific's Northern Express Company. During World War I, all these were combined into one company, American Railway Express, renamed in 1929 as the Railway Express Agency, or REA.[27]

Express business was an essential part of the public's connection to railways. Meredith Willson celebrated this in his musical play (and subsequent film) *The Music Man*, set in Iowa in 1912. Railway express parcels that passenger trains delivered to the depot at the edge of town reached the business district on the Wells Fargo wagon. In a rousing musical number, the townspeople of "River City" line up to greet the Wells Fargo wagon, and individuals sing of remembered items they had earlier received: special foods, clothing, furniture, and other household goods.[28]

Express companies carried money in coin, currency, and other negotiable forms that required special security. On some stations, as in Bozeman, steel bars over the windows indicated the express portion of the building. Express cars had locked safes that were sometimes the target of train robbers. The best-known train robbery in Montana was the last one conducted by members of the famous Wild Bunch, although contrary to some accounts, neither Butch Cassidy nor the Sundance Kid participated. Three men,

Left, detail of a postcard that was sorted and postmarked aboard the Railway Post Office car of Burlington Route train No. 30, Billings to Denver, North Division (Billings to Casper, Wyoming) on July 9, 1967. Note that while the train number is shown, the name of the railroad is not. Less than three months later, with the loss of the mail contract, this train ended service.
Author's collection

including "Kid Curry" (Harvey Logan), stopped and robbed Great Northern train No. 3 just east of Wagner (about seven miles west of Malta) on July 3, 1901, and reportedly got away with about forty thousand dollars.[29] Apparently, Dorothy M. Johnson wrote her short story "The Man Who Knew the Buckskin Kid" with this episode as background.[30]

Railways hauled most of the nation's mail from the mid-nineteenth century into the mid-twentieth century, and this practice continued on main lines into the 1960s. Post offices in towns posted cutoff times when departing mail was taken to the station to be put on a train. Trains carried mail in two forms: in staffed mobile post offices and greater quantities in canvas bags in mail-storage cars.

Many trains included a car housing a mobile post office—a Railway Post Office (RPO)—staffed by employees of the U.S. Post Office. In RPO cars, clerks sorted and postmarked mail while picking up and dropping off mail at nearly every town along the line. When trains stopped at a station, the RPO could briefly serve local purposes. On each side of an RPO car were letter slots through which the public could deposit letters and postcards, knowing that within minutes the mail would be on its way. Major railway stations also had letter boxes on the platforms, from which RPO crews would gather outgoing mail during train stops. All mail cancelled on RPOs was specially marked. Examples include the illustrated envelopes that artist Charlie Russell sent from Great Falls to Butte: HAVRE & ANACONDA R. P. O. / MAR 23 1900 / TR23.[31] This refers to the RPO on Great Northern train 23, at that time a Havre–Great Falls–Helena–Butte run with cars continuing on to Anaconda over the Butte, Anaconda & Pacific Railway.

Local postal workers moved mail directly between a town's post office and the Railway Post Office car at the station platform. During the 1930s, on the Canadian National main line in Semans, Saskatchewan:

> Mr. Bandeen pushed his mail cart to and from the post office each morning and night for many years and many people would rush to hand him a last minute letter or the trainmen on the mail car were very good natured and took letters. Mr. Steenson often sorted the mail at night after train time, especially during [Second World] war years, so there would be a general exit from the station to the post office to see if there would be a letter put in one's box.[32]

The U.S. mail arrived at and left many small towns on main-line trains that did not stop. On the ground by the track was a mail crane, a tall vertical post with arms and brackets that held up a canvas bag of outgoing mail. On the outside of the RPO, a steel hook snagged the bag from the crane while the train passed at full speed, and incoming mailbags were kicked off the train through a doorway.[33] This daily event even attracted observers. During the summer of 1962, a field surveyor with the U.S. Geological Survey, who lived with his family in the small town of Belfield, North Dakota, on the Northern Pacific main line eighty-five miles east of Glendive, reported: "The balance of the summer we used to go to the railroad station in the evening and watch the train [eastbound *North Coast Limited*] roar through town without stopping. They would throw the incoming mailbags off and snatch the outgoing mail with a pickup arm arrangement."[34]

Southern Pacific's San Joaquin Daylight takes northbound mail from Caliente, California, in December 1966 toward Oakland-San Francisco.

Warren McGee, photographer, MHS, PAc 97-93.04401

Great Northern train No. 27—the Fast Mail—heads west out of Libby on April 28, 1941. The train has seven cars of mail and express and two cars for passengers. The Kootenai River is on the left.

The U.S. Post Office contracted with some railroads to run dedicated "mail trains." Carrying few passengers or none at all, these ran on fast schedules with many cars of mail, including an RPO, as well as cars of express and expedited perishables in refrigerated cars. The quantity of goods carried on these trains often made them longer than the better-known passenger expresses. From 1909 to 1960, the Great Northern ran the only such dedicated mail train between Minnesota and Puget Sound. Numbered 27 and 28 and generally called the "Fast Mail," it usually did not appear on public timetables. In the mid-twentieth century, the train included sixteen or more cars of mail and express with a coach at the end for the crew. With its lucrative government contract, the Fast Mail was an operation both prized and carefully monitored by the GN. In 1960, the Great Northern combined the Fast Mail with the secondary transcontinental passenger train *Western Star.*

In his autobiography, Stoyan Christowe recalled his work on a large "extra gang" of immigrant track workers on the plains of northern Montana around 1913. Their task installing new rail created a gap in the track. This gap had to be temporarily bridged with quickly laid rails to allow a train to pass, and the workers paused.

> One man asked, "Why did we close up?"
> Another answered, "I think for the *Fast Mail.* That's the train which carries the U.S. mail from St. Paul to Seattle. It's the fastest train on the line. If Pat [the crew foreman]

> stopped it for one minute we'd have a new boss tomorrow morning. Freight trains you can hold.[35]

As the mail train approached the crew, Christowe imagined what was on the train:

> There were only three mail cars attached to the engine, and these were loaded with letters and packages, with bonds, shares, gold certificates, with jewels and gold, and other precious stuffs. They would be delivered to the doors of houses, or into steam-heated offices in cities on the Coast, and some would be put on steamships to go to the Orient.[36]

Section crews

Assuming, by the late 1960s, that many readers had little familiarity with rail travel, Richard Reinhardt wrote:

> A few years ago, when everyone in America traveled by train, there would have been no need to explain the meaning of the term "section gang." A section gang, as every alert railroad passenger knew, was a group of men—muscular, sunburned, streaked with dust and sweat—who stood along the railroad right-of-way, leaning on crowbars and mallets, and peered at you through the windows of the lounge car as the train slipped cautiously over a newly repaired stretch of track. Section gangs were—and still are—the maintenance crews, the housekeepers of the railroad. . . . When a train comes past, they step aside; and their faces flicker past the window, gazing curiously in while the passengers gaze curiously out.[37]

The section gangs were as much a part of the railroad, whether seen from trains or observed doing their work in towns and cities, as the agent and telegraphers at the station and the familiar crew assigned to the daily local train that regularly stopped in town. Section crews certainly do not get the historical attention given to the larger construction crews, especially those who built main lines from the 1860s into the 1890s. One hundred years ago, these maintenance-of-way employees were more numerous than any other group of railroaders, including those in train service or working in the roundhouses and repair shops. Many men who emigrated to the

United States found their first work in the new land on a track crew. In Montana in 1913, out of a total of about twenty-three thousand railway workers, over ten thousand were track workers. Among the many immigrants on section crews were Italians, Greeks, Japanese, Bulgarians, and Romanians.[38]

The section crew inspected and maintained a length of track usually under ten miles long—its section. The distance was determined by the limits of travel to work sites by hand-pumped two-axle track cars. The workers patrolled the line, performed routine repairs on the track, cleared firebreaks, cleaned ditches and culverts, fixed right-of-way fences, and generally kept the property tidy. In the winter, they cleared snow from cuts, switches, and station platforms. Each crew consisted of a foreman and up to about eight workers from spring to fall and perhaps just a couple of workers in the winter.[39] The larger crews in the summer might include football players from the local high school preparing for the fall season by installing two-hundred-pound wooden crossties.

Townspeople saw crewmen traveling to and from their work on the hand-pump cars, and beginning in the 1910s, some crews used small gasoline-motor "speeder" cars. They were visible when working in town on railway property, including minor carpentry work on the station, loading dock, and stockyard that did not require the attention of the full "bridge and building gang." People knew the small cluster of buildings next to the track where the crew lived and based their work. The section foreman was, along with the station agent, often among the best-known railroaders in small towns. Like the agent, a foreman was sometimes stationed in a town for many years, even decades.

Hal Borland recalled the section foreman in Flagler, Colorado, in the mid-1910s on a Rock Island main line. He was often present where men gathered to visit and talk. In the 1880s,

> Mike Quinn . . . helped build the railroad. And Mike was a veteran of the Civil War. After the rails were laid, he worked for the railroad as a maintenance man, was head of the local section gang for years. He was full of stories about the old days, at least half of them true and all of them rich with Irish wit and Irish brogue. When he told a whopper, most of his listeners knew what it was. . . . But when he talked about how they built the railroad, Mike Quinn was listened to with attention and respect.[40]

A century ago, railroad section work provided the first income for many immigrants. In his novel *Out of This Furnace,* Thomas Bell portrays the range of work done by the main character, Slovak immigrant George Kracha, in eastern Pennsylvania. Kracha's tasks were the same done through decades by section men across the continent:

> He lined and surfaced track, renewed ties, replaced rails, cleaned ditches and culverts, repaired fences, put up cattle guards. During August, before seedtime, he became a farmer again, swinging a scythe on weeds. He learned the names and uses of tools, to recognize cocked joints and broomed rails, to spot a tie that was pumping ballast, to use a Jim Crow, the U-shaped rail bender, to swing a twelve-pound sledge. He fought brush fires in dry weather and floodwater in wet. Storms made silt of ballast, threatened trestles, uprooted trees and telegraph poles; in winter the ballast froze, the switches froze, spikes snapped like glass, snow choked the flangeways, and drifted in white hills across the tracks.[41]

Railroads operated around the clock in all kinds of weather and needed to have certain employees close to their work, especially when unexpected circumstances—heavy snow, a flood or washout, a wreck—might require their presence as quickly as possible. Thus, whether in town or a distance away, the section base was a small cluster of buildings and other features close to the track. The section house was where the foreman and his family lived, and many of these houses were large enough to provide living quarters and meals for the crew. Many railroads had separate bunkhouses for the workers. The standard plans for an NP bunkhouse stated the reason for separate bunkhouses: where crews could not all fit in the section house or where "foreign labor is employed that does its own cooking."[42] On Great Northern station plats from the early twentieth century, bunkhouses specifically for Japanese are labeled, using the casual abbreviation of the time, "Jap. Ho." There was also a variety of smaller buildings, usually a combination of sheds for the handcar or motor speeder, track tools, and coal as well as chicken coops, root cellars, privies ("WC" for "water closet" on railroad station plats), and wells.

When train passengers who were also readers of popular railroad fiction saw these little railroad settlements, they perhaps

Robert C. Morrison, photographer, MHS, R. C. Morrison collection, box 10/1

The hand-pump car was a favorite stage for photographs of track workers, such as this Northern Pacific section crew at the Blatchford section house, twenty-nine miles east of Miles City. The Blatchford standard-plan section house had two bedrooms and a bunk room on the upper floor; on the ground floor, a living room and dining room; and, in a one-story rear extension, a large kitchen. The river cobblestones lining the pathways show the attention that some section foremen put into a place that combined work and residence. Blatchford truly was an isolated section house: there was no telegraph station there.

Photographer unknown, MHS, 2013-50.1240

This postcard of the Great Northern section base at Snowden, on the main line just west of the North Dakota border, carries a message dated August 3, 1912. The crew lived in the two-story section house and smaller bunkhouse by the water tank.

These Japanese workers photographed on a handcar near Butte about 1909 worked on the construction of the Milwaukee Road.

Photographer unknown, MHS, Lot 33 B1.F9.09

thought of stories that featured itinerant ("boomer") telegraph operators working in remote train order stations and sharing their isolation with the section crew. In a story by telegrapher-author Harry Bedwell, published in *Railroad Magazine* in 1940 (with a cover price of fifteen cents), boomer telegrapher Eddie Sand arrives on the local train at his newest assignment, a train order station in the desert of southern California:

> He got off the local and inspected the set-up with satisfaction. . . .
>
> The yellow station looked like a huge desert growth. Section houses, low barracks for the men and their families, a larger structure for the foreman, and a toolhouse, barely broken through the sweep of the desert. Mexican children played on the hard earth, and chattering women gathered in long lines of their eternal washing.[43]

CHAPTER 3

Railroads in the Rural Landscape

WORK ON THE RAILROAD brought certain benefits to employees and their families, including "passes" for free travel on the company's passenger trains. And station agents worked right where the trains stopped. June Pitman was the daughter of a Milwaukee Road station agent who served on the main line in central Montana, at Lombard, Sixteen, and Ringling. "At age 13 [in 1932] she rode the Milwaukee line 150 miles round trip from Ringling to Butte one day a month and took one-hour drum lessons."[1] The round-trip distance was actually 260 miles; the travel time each way—through canyons and over mountains—was about four hours.

The two types of stations that appear most in fiction, film, memoir, and pictorial art are the great urban terminals and the small-town railway depots. Of all the types of station buildings, by far the most numerous was the small-town station. In this station and on the platform between it and the main track, nearly all railway transactions with townspeople and local businesses took place. Stations also hosted the social and celebratory functions associated with the arrival of trains, whether the daily local or the campaign train of a candidate running for office.

The location and size of station buildings was, of course, primarily the result of decisions by the railway companies, but it was also shaped by community and regulatory forces. People in towns often complained about the size, condition (if in poor repair or dirty), or staffing of railway stations. They sought government regulation to strengthen their cases. In 1905, the Montana legislature passed a

Photographer unknown, MHS, PAc 83-33.11

In this photograph taken before 1916, items of express or less-than-carload freight, including milk cans, barrels, a disassembled steel-wheeled hay mower, and a single-cylinder gas engine with large flywheels, sit on the platform of the Great Northern combination passenger-freight station at Broadview, forty-eight miles northwest of Billings. The sign on the telegrapher's bay reads "GREAT NORTHERN EXPRESS CO." The semaphore train order signal for eastbound trains (vertical) is set to "clear" (no stop required), and for westbound trains (horizontal) it is set to "stop." Note the three grain elevators lining the industry track.

law that required railways to build and "maintain facilities for shipment and delivery of freight, and to ship and deliver freight and accommodate passengers at any point upon the line of such railway where there is a platted townsite of record having not less than one hundred inhabitants."[2] Two years later, the state legislature acted again, this time to form a state Board of Railroad Commissioners, an agency with regulatory powers. Citizens and companies presented their cases concerning the railroads' obligation to the traveling public and shippers of freight to the commissioners. In growing towns, citizens' groups or community leaders sometimes appealed directly to the railroads as they tried to convince the company to either expand an existing depot or to build a new larger one.

In Montana and throughout the West, the most common type of station building was the standard-plan combination passenger-freight depot. From the 1880s into the 1910s, railways built tens of thousands of miles of main and branch lines in the West and planned to construct stations at thousands of places. Each railroad employed architects to develop sets of plans based on several factors. A contemporary source noted, "The size is, of course, based upon some estimate of the population of the locality or the amount of business to be had."[3] For example, in small towns, the Great Northern "used one 30' x 48' combination depot plan at more than thirty points between the Twin Cities and Puget Sound."[4] (These sites included two discussed below, at Brady and Zurich.) Railroads employed "bridge and building" (B&B) crews to build and, if necessary, to expand the depots, and section crews did small-scale repairs.

Across the West, the basic standard-plan depot was usually a one-story, wood-frame, gable-roofed building with its long axis parallel to the tracks. The exterior emphasized function over ornamentation. The few attributes that visually differentiated stations between companies usually appeared in details of the roof and eaves or decoration in the gable ends. One historian of depots noted, "The distinctive features of country railroad stations in the trans-Mississippi West are easily described. While important exceptions exist, their most notable characteristics are cheapness, frame construction, replicable rather than unique design, and utility."[5]

The most basic interior plan had three components: the office, the passenger waiting room, and the freight room. The office, with a projecting windowed bay, combined many functions: ticket sales and baggage checking for passengers, express shipping, freight business transactions, telegraph operations, and maintaining a great array of paperwork and records documenting all the station's activities. In the freight room, with large doors for baggage trucks, less-than-carload freight was unloaded, sorted, or loaded into boxcars. Freight included that received in wooden boxes or crates: items such as furniture, parts for farm equipment and other machinery, large household appliances, bulky items for businesses, and more. Freight in larger carload lots was loaded or unloaded either at heavy wooden freight docks or at spur tracks next to the business customers.

Many western stations included living quarters for the station agent and family. From the railroad's viewpoint, having agents living next to their work had several benefits. It encouraged married agents, considered more reliable workers than single men, to take work in communities where private housing was either scarce or primitive. Inhabited stations also reduced both the premiums for fire insurance and the likelihood of robbery or vandalism.[6]

Standard-plan stations with living quarters were fairly common. The Milwaukee Road had a floor plan for a one-story depot with dimensions of twenty-four by sixty feet with living quarters—sitting room, kitchen, and bedroom—in the central part of the building, between the waiting room and office on one side and the freight room on the other. On the plan sheet were listed the seven places in Montana with such depots.[7] The NP had a plan for a two-story depot with living quarters on the second floor, which was less than half the size of the first floor. The quarters consisted of two bedrooms, a kitchen, and a living room directly above the office, with the windowed telegrapher's bay extending upward to it. At least eleven station buildings based on this plan were erected in Montana.[8]

Standard-plan depots included larger buildings that had additional internal divisions, creating separate express or baggage rooms or a separate women's waiting room. But indoor plumbing was absent from many standard-plan depots. Often there were no indoor toilet facilities for passengers, staff, and the resident agent and family. Instead, an outdoor privy served that need. Each

Photographer unknown, MHS, PAc 2313-59.1158

This photograph postcard of the Minneapolis, St. Paul & Sault Ste. Marie Railway, better known as the Soo Line, shows the station at Dooley in far northeastern Montana. The station is one of the railway's standard-plan "second class" two-story buildings. The second story has two bedrooms, a kitchen, and living room for the agent's family. The unsigned message on the back of the postcard, postmarked in August 1919, explains the Xs on the photo: "This cross is where I set my cream can and one is where I tie my horse and the other on[e] is where they set the empty can." On the platform is a lever scale on small wheels for weighing express and smaller items of less-than-carload freight.

Elizabeth C. Nixon, photographer, MOR RVN 33052

Six-year-old Ron V. Nixon and his brother play on the platform of their home, the Northern Pacific station at Roberts, forty-seven miles southwest of Billings on the branch line to Red Lodge, in 1917. The boys' parents were telegraph operators for the NP, and the family lived in the small-town stations where they worked. Ron's mother taught him photography, a skill he used throughout his life to document railroad history.

company had standard plans for privies, with either one or two holes, for the stations and the employees in dwellings and bunkhouses within the right-of-way.

The Station Agent

The station agent, almost always a man, was an important person for the railroad and in the town. He combined the responsibilities of the company's local manager and sales representative and was often a respected community member. In a branch line depot, the agent was probably the only employee and thus was also ticket clerk, baggage checker, telegrapher, express agent, and freight handler, all of which required large amounts of paperwork. Each agent was part of a vast enterprise with business in hundreds of places and was responsible for daily operations, with information on each transaction to be recorded on a specific form from among dozens of standard forms. Furthermore, the agent compiled weekly and monthly summaries of all types of transactions and sent them to corporate headquarters. Traveling auditors visited to check on the agent's work and records.

The tasks of the agent at the Great Northern station at Brady, on the secondary main line between Great Falls and Shelby, are detailed in that town's published history:

David Plowden, photographer, courtesy David Plowden, Beinecke Library, Yale University, New Haven, CT, WA MSS 5-2957

Agent Ray H. Birkhead is shown here in the Missouri-Kansas-Texas Railroad (M-K-T) station at Frederick, Oklahoma, in July 1968. When photographer David Plowden stopped there, Birkhead said that it was his last day of work after sixty years with M-K-T. The photograph shows the spartan interior and lighting of the station, the many niches in the desk for the multitude of forms for which an agent was responsible, and an upside-down spike bucket behind Birkhead's legs.

> The station agent copied train orders from the train dispatcher to deliver to the trains, made switch lists for the local freight [train] to switch cars in the yard, handled Western Union Telegraph messages, sold passenger tickets, handled baggage, milk and cream shipments, less than carload freight, carload freight, railway express shipments, etc. Looking up the rates and charges for these services plus the waybilling, expensing, and accounting that had to be done for each one, kept an agent very busy.[9]

Some agents worked for years or even decades in one place and were among the best known and most respected men in town. In mid-twentieth-century Scobey, in far northeastern Montana, Fred Haun had served as the Great Northern's agent for more than three decades. An article in the town's thirty-fifth anniversary book (1948) described him:

> Dean of the Great Northern railway employees in this part of the west, Fred Haun, Scobey's genial depot agent for more than 30 years past. . . . Long past retirement time in service, Fred is still going strong and certainly no G. N. patron here wants him to quit. He's as much a part of Scobey as the postoffice.

The article reported Haun's service in community organizations, his military service, and that of his son.[10]

Zurich, Montana, on the Great Northern Railway

In the late 1910s, Zurich was a small, unincorporated community in Blaine County, thirty-one miles east of Havre on the Great Northern transcontinental main line. Zurich began as a station with a telegraph office on the Manitoba Road's Montana Extension in 1888, and it remained a minor railway point for twenty years. The town developed after 1908 when the GN began vigorous promotion of dry-land farming in northern Montana as well as irrigated farming along the Milk River, which flowed just south of town. The platted streets of Zurich were aligned like those of many other settlements established along rail lines: parallel and perpendicular to the main line track, not conventionally oriented north-south and east-west.

Detail, photographer unknown, MHS, Lot 28-B1 F8.1

An employee of the Montana State Highway Department took this photo, looking east from the west edge of Zurich in April 1922, to show the condition of the grandly named Theodore Roosevelt International Highway running east-west across northern Montana, today's U.S. Route 2. The photographer also captured the Great Northern station and section base. The station is the closest major building, with the small privy barely discernible closer to the foreground. Beyond the station sits the one-and-a-half-story section house and behind that, the roof and back wall of the bunkhouse for Japanese track workers. Two pole lines stand between the road and railway. Three grain elevators line the industry track.

Zurich was located near the center of a large trade area, approximately fifty miles from north to south and ten to twelve miles east to west, situated between the hinterlands of the larger towns of Chinook (the county seat) to the west and Harlem to the east. In 1920, the Montana Board of Railroad Commissioners estimated Zurich's town population to be about one hundred.[11]

In the spring of 1917, one of the businesses in Zurich had a new owner. The father of eight-year-old Dan Cushman "bought a pool hall and dance hall" that "was clubroom for the whole town—population 75."[12] Located across the street from the railway station, it offered a view of the community's railway activity. The Cushman family moved into part of the building that housed the combination pool hall–soda fountain and dance hall. Dan and his family lived in Zurich until the autumn of 1918, when they moved to Havre. Written in 1975, Dan Cushman's memoir, *Plenty of Room & Air*, included a portrait of Zurich and the Great Northern Railway.

Perhaps the most architecturally distinctive part of a small town was the railway station windowed bay facing the track. Built into the bay was a table where the telegraph operator worked, with a view straight ahead and of the track in both directions. The table held the instruments of communications linked to several telegraph and telephone circuits, including the keys for sending Morse code and, mounted on movable arms, the "sounders" that clicked received messages. The sounders were often placed in wooden boxes to amplify them. In this setting, Cushman recalled a quiet day at the GN station in Zurich: "It was just a regular peaceful, quiet day, not a thing stirring. . . . It was so quiet Huttinger, the depot agent would swing his telegraph arm to the open window, and then go and sit in

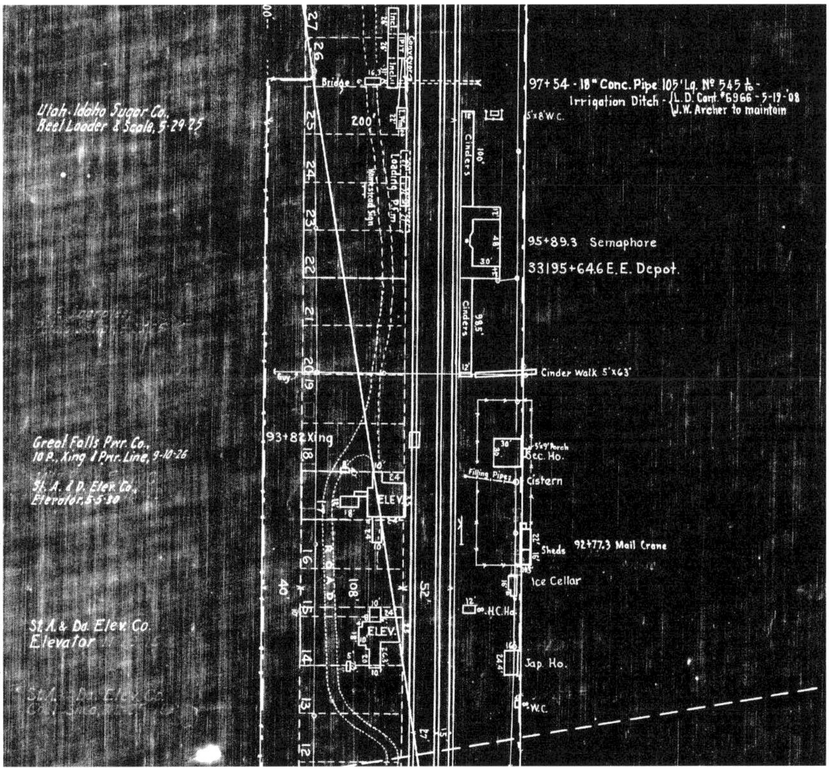

Montana Department of Transportation

Detail from the Great Northern Railway station plat for Zurich, with a scale of 1 inch = 100 feet on the original (issued in 1919 and revised in 1936–37). The lettering is oriented with west at the top. The depot and section base, with associated buildings and structures, are shown, as well as two of the three grain elevators.

the privy 50 yards away and be able to read any message that clicked in on the sounder."[13]

The type and function of GN buildings and structures within the right-of-way at Zurich were typical of railway properties at thousands of towns across North America. The Great Northern Railway's station plat map of Zurich, dated 1919 and revised in 1936–37, documents the numerous features the company had established there.[14] The features that justified all the rest were the tracks, which included the main line, a passing siding, and an industry track for shippers of bulk commodities. The station building was on the north side of the tracks, literally and functionally between the town and rail line. It was a standard-plan structure, thirty by forty-eight feet, similar to those in at least half a dozen other small, unincorporated communities on GN's Hi-Line.[15] The station privy, from which the agent could hear the telegraph sounder on quiet days, was at the west end of the 265-foot-long station platform of cinders within wood curbs. Beyond the east end of the platform was the mail crane, from which outgoing mailbags were snatched by long-distance trains that passed without stopping. Across the tracks from the station was a feature labeled "Homestead Sign" on the plat map. This sign encouraged settlement along the GN.

Zurich was the base for the section crew that maintained about ten miles of main line track and associated sidings and spurs. The primary buildings of the base, just east of the station, were two dwellings: the one-and-a-half-story foreman's house, which may have included quarters for some of the crew, and a separate bunkhouse for Japanese workers. There were also privies, one shed for supplies and another for the track car that was the crew's vehicle, a cistern, and an ice cellar.

West of the station stood the water facility for filling locomotive tenders. It included a one-hundred-thousand-gallon tank, a gas motor pump at the well in the pump house, a treatment plant to remove dissolved minerals from the water, and a dwelling and privy for the "pumper" who operated and maintained the plant. The GN initially stored water in an earthen-dammed reservoir, which was abandoned in 1933 and replaced by the well.

Along the industry track were the businesses that provided most of the income that the GN earned at Zurich. The station plat shows three grain elevators: two of the St. Anthony & Dakota Elevator Company, which located all of its elevators along the GN, and one of the Imperial Elevator Company. The Utah & Idaho Sugar Company shipped out beets grown on irrigated land along the Milk River from a "beet loader" on the industry track. There was also a railroad-owned stockyard and chute for loading livestock into railcars.

In mid-January 1920, a U.S. Census enumerator visited Zurich and recorded the presence of, and information on, the residents, including six employees of the Great Northern. Working in the station were two men: the station agent and daytime telegraph operator William Huttinger (mentioned by Cushman) and another operator, who presumably worked a second shift. Both were born in the United States and had families. The section foreman was an immigrant from the Austro-Hungarian Empire and a native speaker of Serbian. In subsequent censuses, he was employed as section foreman in 1930 at Chinook, and by 1940 he had returned to Zurich. At Zurich in January 1920, the foreman oversaw a crew reduced during winter to just two laborers. One was the foreman's father-in-law, an immigrant from Belgium, and the other was a native of Minnesota. Finally, tending the water tank was the "water pumper" and his family. The census manuscript did not record whether these employees lived in the company-provided housing shown on the GN's station plat.[16]

Young Dan Cushman got to see and know railway workers. Sometimes a freight train took the siding at Zurich to get out of the way of higher priority trains. Then the trainmen would "leave the train on a siding, and loaf around our pool hall. They might be there the whole afternoon if a number of through trains had clearance, until Huttinger, the station agent, hustled over to give them their orders and they'd highball for the division point at Bodoin [Bowdoin], making up for lost time."[17]

Also stopping at Zurich, for much longer, were work trains. These were bases for large crews ("extra gangs") that did major repair tasks on the tracks and related structures. Each crew, often including many recent immigrants, lived on a "work train" composed of old passenger and freight cars adapted for housing and supplies and parked close to their work. Cushman recalled:

> Work trains often stopped at Zurich for weeks at a time, a pleasant place with a mile of siding in the cool cottonwoods along Milk River. When there was no work for

> them . . . the men sat around in the shade, talking foreign tongues, and some of them flew kites. It was a great place for kites; the wind blew every day all day and beyond Milk River bottoms no visible limit but prairie and boundless sky. They flew kites out of sight. I wanted a kite, too.[18]

World War I brought war fears and hysteria concerning the immigrant workers on one extra gang. Later, Cushman turned it into a humorous story. The station agent received "a warning to all points along the line that an extra gang had taken over a work train; the gang, 100 strong, was composed of Austrians and Bulgarians, both allies of Germany; they were flying the Austrian and Bulgarian flags; they were armed to the teeth; and people who attempted to approach the train were being fired on." The deputy sheriff at Harlem and several other men found the extra gang at the siding of Matador.

> There was the work train, all quiet. Everybody seemed to be sitting around in the shade. Cautious approach, no ambush. A search of the train yielded two old side-hammer shotguns. The gang proved to be Greek, not Bulgarian. There were flags on the cars, one the flag of Greece and one the flag of the United States. Greece was our ally. There'd been shooting, all right. A cook's helper had been hunting and killed a duck. The duck was confiscated. The deputy didn't return empty handed. He took the cook's helper into custody, transported him to Harlem, where he was fined $10 for hunting out of season. So ended the Austro-Bulgarian invasion of June 1917.[19]

The Skidoo

The primary transportation to and from Zurich provided by the Great Northern was a local train called the Skidoo. Most of the passenger trains passed through Zurich without stopping. The one pair of trains that did stop was the Skidoo operated through most of the first half of the twentieth century.

The Skidoo apparently acquired its nickname from a popular phrase of the first half of the twentieth century. The westbound train, No. 223, fit with a phrase very popular at that time—"23 skidoo." The word "skidoo" and phrase "23 skidoo" had similar meanings: "to go away, leave, or depart hurriedly" or to "scram."[20]

Great Northern train No. 223, known locally as the "Skidoo," arrives in Havre on May 2, 1940, after completing its run of ten hours and twenty minutes for the 310 miles from Williston, North Dakota. The train consists of a mail car, two express refrigerator cars (an unusual presence on this train), an express-baggage car, and a day coach.

Warren McGee, photographer, MHS, PAc 97-93.05684

For a short time around 1907, the GN operated a pair of passenger trains between St. Paul and Havre that made many more stops across Minnesota, North Dakota, and northeastern Montana than the transcontinental trains. The trains, numbered 23 and 24, were unnamed in the timetable. The pair of trains quickly acquired the nickname Skidoo.[21]

Playing on the meaning of "skidoo" as reckless haste, a contemporary journal noted briefly: "Great Northern train No. 23, known as the 'Skidoo Special,' was wrecked recently. Still some people say there is nothing in a name or number."[22] Through subsequent changes in terminals and train numbers (soon settling on Nos. 223 and 224), the nickname stuck. The train usually consisted of a steam locomotive and two or three cars carrying head-end traffic (express and mail), a smoking compartment or car, and a day coach. Two stories, three decades apart, portray examples of the use of this train.

In February 1913, Polly Bertino and Aldo Vaira rode the Skidoo to their wedding, departing from the bride's family homestead.

People, Stations, and Trains

Many historical photos of people at railway stations were taken for reasons that will likely never be known. In many cases, the station building was the setting for an event that involved the travel of the people pictured, or those gathered were awaiting the arrival or had seen the departure of passengers not in the photo. Some photos may also be the products of traveling photographers, working for the railroad or self-employed, who sought individuals to appear in their images. Rarely are those present in the photos identified by name or as townspeople, visitors, railroaders, or individuals of local or greater importance. There are almost always men in the photos—women and children may be absent or present in small numbers. Aside from the people photographed, there are often baggage trucks loaded with luggage, mail, and express, and barrels, crated materials, and other objects left by less-than-carload freight. Horse-pulled or motor vehicles are often stopped near the depot.

In the photos that follow, the reader is invited to wonder: Who are the people? What event or purpose has brought them (and the photographer) to the depot?

A cold, late spring day at Lennep, on the Milwaukee Road main line west of Harlowton, on June 10, 1915 Thomas E. Sorboe, photographer, MOR x75.3.2438

Ron V. Nixon, photographer, MOR RVN 34251

The “station force” at Gardiner during the summer tourist season in 1927

F. Jay Haynes, photographer, MHS, H-3113

Railroad photographer F. Jay Haynes took this photograph of the Northern Pacific passenger station at Miles City in 1894. The men may be either waiting for a train or gathered just for the photo.

Ron V. Nixon, photographer, MOR RVN 06348

Laurel, fifteen miles west of Billings, was a junction and switchyard. Train time is shown here as eastbound No. 4 arrives and a horse-drawn hotel transfer wagon awaits.

Photographer unknown, MHS, PAc 74-104.148GP

This photograph appears to be of a family group at the Northern Pacific station at the mining town of Elkhorn, southeast of Helena. The name of the station on the wall behind the group is almost completely hidden under the roof.

The Great Northern station at Flaxville, in northeastern Montana, with a mixed freight-passenger train headed west toward Scobey. At the end of the train, behind several boxcars, is a combination baggage-coach.

Photographer(s) unknown, MHS, (above) PAc 2013-50.1165, (below) 957-373

Stenographers from Butte at Big Timber, seat of Sweet Grass County, in 1913. The women came to copy local government records—especially pertaining to land and ownership—for the eastern part of Sweet Grass County that would become the western part of newly created Stillwater County, with its seat at Columbus. Such work was a necessary and common aspect of the creation of many new counties during the era of the homestead boom in the 1910s.

(following pages) Ron Nixon photographed the Laurel station's staff in 1950.
Ron V. Nixon, photographer, MOR RVN 16233

LAUREL

This special train stopped for a large group photograph on March 16, 1885, at Gallatin, Montana, close to the Missouri River headwaters. The large snowplow on the front of the locomotive provides additional seating.
Photographer unknown, MHS, Lot 33 B3/F8.01

The small station at Jefferson Island, forty-eight miles east of Butte, is dwarfed by the tall train order signal. The four handcars, each with scoop shovels and other tools, convey mobilization for a task that required more people than a normal section crew. The railroad is identified by the lettering on the handcars: C.M.&St.P.Ry (Chicago, Milwaukee & St. Paul Railway).

Photographer unknown, MHS, PAc 2013-50.1200

Photographer unknown, MHS, PAc 98-57.16

A crowd awaits the arrival of the special train bringing President Theodore Roosevelt to Butte on the Great Northern Railway from Helena on May 27, 1903. At this time, GN passenger trains in Butte used the Butte, Anaconda & Pacific Railway station. The central and western portions of the building housed freight handling and storage, thus the lettering on the west wall. The passenger function is out of view at the east end but is represented in the platform shed roof in the right background.

"In Brockton, they flagged down the 'skidoo, a local railway train with two cars, one for passengers and the other for cream cans and other freight.' They took the train, which 'stopped at every town and anywhere between towns if flagged down,' to Glasgow [eighty-five miles from Brockton], where the wedding was performed."[23]

Three decades later, the local train still served and stopped as needed. During World War II, rationing of gasoline and tires brought some passengers back to the Skidoo. In a blog post, "Skidoo Kid" told two stories of growing up on a farm close to the dwindling settlement of Coburg, twenty-eight miles west of Malta, and riding the Skidoo. When she was nine, she rode the train because her chores included the "job of going eleven miles from Coburg to Dodson for the mail or any grocery item that my parents might need." Her second story details how one "flagged" or stopped a local train.

> On this day when I was 9 years old I knelt on the railroad track and put my ear to the rail. The distant sound of the steam locomotive echoed down the track. When I saw the engine emerge from around the bend to the west I stood in the middle of the track, waving my arms up and down until the "toot, toot" assured me that I had been seen. As the steam locomotive pulling two cars came to a grinding stop, the conductor, stepped down and placed a stool for me.

On her return trip, she "asked the conductor to let me off at the crossing west of the Coburg depot so I could walk across our alfalfa field to our farm home . . . and save a little walking time. He contacted the engineer and they obligingly stopped."[24]

The Skidoo lasted into the early 1950s, when the Great Northern successfully petitioned the Montana Public Service Commission to end its operation. While replacement buses did stop in Zurich, they passed without pausing at many other places that had been served by the train.[25]

Inconvenient Public Transport, Connections, and Lodging

The passenger travel issues facing many small towns on rail main lines in the United States are represented by the circumstances in Zurich. The number of trains on a schedule often conveyed the appearance of more travel options than were actually available. Some long-distance trains did not stop, and some that stopped did so between late evening and early morning. The schedule of local trains often favored travel in one direction over the other.

The Great Northern schedule at Zurich in the timetable for July 1920 illustrated the difficulties of living with schedules designed for railway convenience and for trains based at distant terminals. The Skidoo stopped at Zurich eastbound in the morning and westbound in the late afternoon. Thus, round-trips within one day were possible to larger towns with better shopping and commercial options to the east, such as Harlem, ten miles away. To the west, however, even a short-distance round-trip by train required overnight stays. Chinook, the county seat just nine miles to the west, was a common destination for people boarding the train in Zurich. Of course, "the traveler bent on county seat business" needed to be in Chinook while offices were open. A trip from Zurich to Chinook on the Skidoo required a late afternoon trip west on the first day, arriving in Chinook after business hours and staying overnight there. The second day, all day, was spent there, even if only a few hours were needed, and then another overnight. On the third day, the return train to Zurich departed before business hours. Altogether, a trip like this required thirty-nine hours and two nights away. In 1920, the people of Zurich petitioned the state railroad commission to get the Great Northern to stop its secondary long-distance trains—Nos. 3 and 4—at Zurich to offer more options in departures and arrivals. The commission agreed and ordered the GN to stop the trains when requested. The improved schedule was slightly more convenient but still required a departure from Zurich at 12:35 A.M. with an abridged overnight in Chinook. The traveler had most of a business day in Chinook before returning to Zurich, "having completed the movement [round-trip and business day in Chinook] in less than eighteen hours."[26] It is not difficult to see why automobiles on improved roads in the 1920s drew short-distance passengers off trains like the Skidoo.

Hotels were a necessary and sometimes annoying component of travel by rail, and hotels close to railway stations in cities and small towns drew much of their business from rail travelers. As with airport hotels now, hotels then served individuals, families, and groups at each end of a journey. Another major part of a hotel's business came from traveling salesmen, formally called "commercial travelers," or informally, "drummers." Drummers represented wholesale firms and manufacturers to retail merchants in the towns of their sales districts, carrying sample cases of hardware, dry goods, groceries, or promotional materials for agricultural equipment and supplies. Sinclair Lewis, in his novel *Free Air*, remarked that "drummers were always to be seen in soggy hotels and badly connecting trains and the headachy waiting-rooms of stations."[27] On trains, they usually rode in the "smoker"—the coach or part of a car set aside for men to smoke cigars. There, they gathered, talked business, swapped stories, smoked and drank, and played cards in an atmosphere that many women found unpleasant or even threatening. A sanitized version is presented in the opening scene of Meredith Willson's musical *The Music Man*.

Hotels also provided travelers with rooms for overnight stays required by layovers or missed connections. Making connections at transport terminals and junctions has been a concern for travelers since the beginning of scheduled passenger transportation. It can be especially worrisome trying to make connections between uncoordinated schedules of different carriers. Layovers may be either too short and close or too long and tedious. Travelers need also be concerned about the presence, and quality, of provisions for rest and food.

An instance of these concerns occurred at the now-vanished settlement of Lombard, on the Missouri River a little downstream from its headwaters, where, after 1910, the main line of the Milwaukee Road crossed over that of the Northern Pacific and offered connections. In 1920, Lombard had a population of just a couple dozen people. Both railways maintained staffed stations there, a few hundred feet apart, with an outdoor elevator to move trucks of baggage and express between the higher Milwaukee station platform and that of the lower NP line. It was an important transfer point for those traveling between stations on the Milwaukee in the upper Musselshell River country (including the towns of Harlowton, Roundup, and Ryegate) as well as Lewistown farther north and points on the NP, in particular, Helena. As the state capital, Helena was a primary travel destination. It was the location of dozens of federal and state government bureaus, offices, and courts as well as the site of the annual state fair and many conventions every year (106 in 1918).

The uncoordinated schedules of passenger trains on the

The daily life of the traveling salesmen revolved around train stations and nearby hotels. Both appear in this view, looking east, of Drummond, forty-eight miles east of Missoula, taken on November 26, 1920. The Northern Pacific station is on the right, with a refrigerator car parked by the freight platform. Front Street is in the center. The white upright feature at the end of the street is the recently installed memorial to John Mullan, who supervised the construction of the 1850s government road across the Rockies. Part of the business district is on the left. The two-story brick Palace Hotel, clearly identified for arriving travelers with a large painted sign, had twenty-two rooms, a café, drugstore, and—before statewide prohibition went into effect on the last day of 1918—a saloon.

Milwaukee and NP at Lombard often made changing trains difficult. From the beginning of regular service on the Milwaukee in 1910, passengers complained to the Board of Railroad Commissioners about the poor connections. In 1915, an organization of traveling salesmen—the Grand Council, Montana, Utah, and Idaho United Commercial Travelers—filed a complaint over inconvenient schedules. In 1920, the railroad commissioners took up the situation. Eastbound travelers had a reasonable connection at Lombard, but travelers going west to Helena had a layover from their arrival on the Milwaukee at 6:50 P.M. to departure on the NP at 6:12 A.M. Those unwilling to wait all night in "the small stove-heated waiting rooms of either carrier" ended up at the

> low frame structure misnamed a hotel. Here only two or three beds may be had and the record plainly shows that, as a lodging house, the place fails to meet the minimum

Robert H. Graham, photographer, MOR RVN 08839

of decency, much less approach the norm of comfort. The two or three travelers who can be sheltered thereat must always tolerate grave inconvenience and many times endure real suffering.

Some passengers traveled farther, at greater expense, to spend overnight in a less unpleasant place, such as Three Forks or Butte. After reviewing the issue, the commissioners ordered the two railroads to revise their schedules to make a convenient connection at Lombard in the early evening, with the NP holding its train to Helena up to fifteen minutes if the Milwaukee train was a little late.[28]

Departures and Life Changes

The country railroad station was, of course, the point of many departures and arrivals. For many rural youth, however, it was often the point of departure of great significance as they left their hometown to begin adult life in a place far enough away to preclude frequent returns. They left for reasons that might have been a combination of work, college, military service, still undetermined adventure, or escape from small-town life. Hal Borland (born 1900) spent his middle teen and high school years (1915–18) in the small town of Flagler, on the eastern plains of Colorado. The rail line through Flagler was the Chicago-Omaha-Denver main line of the Chicago, Rock Island & Pacific Railway. His father owned and edited one of the town's two weekly newspapers. The area was flourishing due to a boom combining dry-land farming with high wartime wheat prices.

In his memoir *Country Editor's Boy,* Borland recalls the prominent role of the Rock Island Line in the town. He mentions the

Photographer unknown, MHS, 97-93.14286

The junction settlement of Lombard is pictured here circa 1908–09. Lombard got its start when the Montana Railroad built its line eastward from a connection with the Northern Pacific main line along the Missouri River fifty-four miles east of Helena. The Montana Railroad's line went up Sixteenmile Creek toward the center of the state. When the Milwaukee Road acquired the Montana Railroad as part of building a transcontinental line, it bridged the Missouri at Lombard. The flatcars in the Montana Railroad switchyard are carrying deck girders for the uncompleted bridge shown at the left edge of the photo. The hotel that became a notorious lodging in subsequent years is the two-story, gable-roofed building in front of the left end of the rocky cliff.

depot but does not describe it. Perhaps for readers of his generation, a small-town depot of unremarkable appearance did not merit further attention in his writing. Borland tells of the arrival and departure of trains carrying family, friends, and mail. A sequence of arrivals, over several days, brought to Flagler the setup crew and performers of the regional Chautauqua show that spent three days there. He worked part of one summer on a temporary crew digging trenches and placing pipe to improve the railroad's water supply system. Borland also conveys the social importance of two railroad employees in the town—the station agent and the section crew foreman. Just after finishing high school in 1918, he left Flagler, going east to a summer job before entering university in the fall.[29] In subsequent decades, he became a journalist and the author of many books, well known for his writing on the natural landscape and world.

Borland ends his memoir with his departure from Flagler, headed to the summer job in Nebraska, looking back from the vestibule at the rear end of the train:

> I stood in the vestibule for a last look, first to the north, at Flagler slipping past, then to the south, out across the old flats that had been the frontier and now were just the High Plains, where a new breed of men were plowing the grass and fencing the wind, or trying to, and making the memories of yesterday the legends of tomorrow.
>
> Then the porter took my suitcase and led the way to my seat. The locomotive, far up there ahead, whistled a long, screaming blast for the crossing a mile east of town. . . . On toward Seibert, Stratton, Burlington, Goodland. East. Toward tomorrow, whatever and wherever it might be.[30]

Lima, Montana

For almost a century, Lima was a small railroad town in far southwestern Montana, located in a high, open valley at an elevation of 6,258 feet. The Union Pacific created Lima to serve as a division point on its main line between Pocatello, Idaho, 146 miles to the south, and Butte, Montana, 116 miles to the north. These distances were one day's work for train crews into the mid-twentieth century. Crews and locomotives changed at Lima. It also was the base for helper engines that assisted trains up to the Continental Divide at Monida Pass, 540 feet higher in elevation and 15 miles to the south. In 1920, less than a decade after formal incorporation, the town had a population of 476.

For three-quarters of the twentieth century, Lima was the Union Pacific's primary base in Montana for employees, operations, and maintenance. In the early decades, many of the locomotives and cars bore the name or initials of the UP subsidiary that operated in southern Idaho and Montana: the Oregon Short Line. In 1898, UP leased its terminal properties in Butte to the Northern Pacific while retaining a minor portion for its own use. Lima then acquired greater importance as the only operating base in Montana fully owned and managed by the UP. At Lima, the Union Pacific had buildings and facilities necessary to support operations, maintain and repair locomotives and cars, and provide lodging, food, and wholesome entertainment to employees. The main structures included a twelve-stall locomotive roundhouse with attached machine and boiler repair shops, a seventy-foot turntable in a circular pit, coaling chutes (a high point good for taking photographs), a water tank, and car repair buildings and tracks. For the employees, the UP provided housing and a clubhouse.

Photographer unknown, MHS, PAc 80-17.21

Overview of Lima, from a height southeast of town, circa 1900. The roundhouse and engine terminal facilities, with the tall chimney, are in the right part of the photo. On the far left is an orderly row of railroad housing.

W. T. Cheney, photographer, MHS, PAc 80-17.29

View to the southeast, from the coaling facility, 1910–12, showing the locomotive turntable, water tank, and railroad housing.

In the early twentieth century, W. T. Cheney worked for the Union Pacific in Lima as a car inspector and foreman and as operator of the crane that was part of the work train that cleaned up after wrecks and other accidents. Cheney's photographs, taken during the first two decades of the century, show the town, railroad properties, operations, and employees at work and in company facilities for entertainment and food.

From the 1930s, railroad operations at Lima gradually diminished as economic changes reduced traffic and new railroad technology required fewer workers. Crews changed at Lima until 1976, when the few remaining railroad functions moved to Dillon.

W. T. Cheney, photographer, MHS, PAc 80-17.27

View to the south in about 1910–12, with the water tank and orderly rows of railroad housing on each side of the tracks. The Lima Peaks form the skyline.

Another view from the coaling tower looks toward the southwest, 1910–12. The station is at far left, and the school is on the right edge of the photo.

W. T. Cheney, photographer, MHS, (top) PAc 80-17.26, (bottom) PAc 80-17.54

Roundhouse and shop workers pose on a locomotive, 1917–18. Steam locomotives provided a convenient stage for group portraits of engine terminal workers. The locomotive is under repair, with part of the boiler just ahead of the cab exposed after the removal of the jacket and insulation.

This steam engine is undergoing repair. To the right of the cab, the sheet-metal boiler jacket and underlying insulation have been removed to reveal the boiler wall with lines of bolts. The men may be roundhouse or shop workers.

W. T. Cheney, photographer, MHS, (top) PAc 80-17.52, (bottom) PAc 80-17.48

In some division points, the railroad provided facilities for their employees' meals and entertainment. The new recreation room in the Lima railroad clubhouse is shown in 1917–18. The signs on the wall in back read "Please keep off the pool tables" and "No loud vulgar or profane language allowed."

The patched tents and wagons of a circus are shown at Lima, circa 1917–18.
W. T. Cheney, photographer, MHS, PAc 80-17.30

W. T. Cheney, photographer, MHS, PAc 80-17.49

The counter, with settings of napkins and flatware, in the dining room in the Oregon Short Line club-house was photographed in 1917.

CHAPTER 4

Urban Terminals

IN 1916, John A. Droege, an official of the New York, New Haven & Hartford Railroad, observed, "The passenger terminal has been aptly described as the city gate and for some of the newer and larger stations it would, indeed, be hard to find a term more fitting."[1]

Great Falls's City Gates

Looking from the west bank of the Missouri River eastward toward the oldest part of the city of Great Falls, two brick towers rise above the nearly solid front of trees on the opposite bank. The towers are less than one-quarter mile apart, and the left (north) tower is the taller and thinner of the two. These towers are part of buildings that were the passenger stations of the two railroads that served Great Falls for much of the twentieth century.

The Manitoba Road, predecessor of the Great Northern Railway, was the first rail line to arrive in Great Falls, in 1887, and the GN remained the dominant railway in the city. After 1909, two routes linking the transcontinental main line in the north with cities in southern Montana intersected here: Havre-Butte and Shelby-Billings. This junction made Great Falls a logical place for the GN to have a large switchyard and major repair shops, where workers both repaired and assembled locomotives. By the 1910s, the Great Northern station complex included the depot building itself and, just to the north, an express building and a commissary building with supplies for the dining cars, buffet cars, and parlor

Ron V. Nixon, photographer, MOR RVN 12578

In this February 11, 1947, photograph taken at the Great Northern passenger station at Great Falls, one of the new streamlined *Empire Builder* trains stands available for public viewing before going into regular service between Chicago and Seattle on February 23. Travelers from Great Falls had to go to Havre or Shelby to ride the *Empire Builder*.

Warren McGee, photographer, MHS, PAc 97-93.04353

Among those trains that stopped at the Great Northern station in Great Falls in 1941 was a pair of unnamed trains operating between Billings and the transcontinental main line at Shelby. The westbound No. 43 curves along the Sun River approaching Manchester, eight miles west of Great Falls, on April 24, 1941. Because it is too early in the season for Glacier Park tourists, there are just three cars on No. 43: one of mail and express, a coach, and a Pullman observation–sleeping car originating in Omaha on a Burlington Route train.

Photographer unknown, The History Museum, Great Falls, 1992.001.0104

The Milwaukee Road passenger station at Great Falls, looking east from the bridge over the Missouri River

cars. At this time, a host of intrastate passenger trains and one pair of Kansas City–Seattle trains stopped, originated, or terminated at GN's passenger station in Great Falls. By 1916, the station saw eighteen passenger trains daily, with destinations that included Butte, Billings, Lewistown, Havre (with connections to St. Paul and Chicago), the Canadian border north of Shelby, Seattle, and Kansas City.[2]

As Droege noted, "The American railroads have frequently been criticized for having lavished such great amounts of money on their passenger stations."[3] This observation seems to be true of the other depot in Great Falls. Tracks of the Milwaukee Road reached Great Falls in 1914, and two years later its station saw just one pair of daily passenger trains, on the run between Great Falls, Lewistown, and the transcontinental main line at Harlowton. By 1920, there were four daily Milwaukee trains, still a small fraction of GN's traffic, with the addition of a pair of mixed freight-passenger trains on the branch line to Agawam, to the northwest.[4]

Large Station Buildings

The large stations in major cities were the most visible and prominent properties of railroads. In Montana, companies built stations of this type in the five largest cities, in smaller towns and cities with "division headquarters," where railroads based administration and operations along main lines, and major tourist gateways, especially for national parks.

Several characteristics defined the major urban terminals. They were usually not subject to the frugal impulses with which railroads planned and built most small-town depots. The terminals built in the early twentieth century, which replaced smaller and generally less distinctive buildings, were large in exterior mass and interior spaces, with façades of masonry—brick, stone, tile, and ornamental terra-cotta. In some cases, the railroad created a park with grass and perhaps trees next to the building. The interior was centered

Photographer unknown, Yellowstone Gateway Museum, Livingston, 2006.044.6859

A group of women and one child gather at the ticket window in this interior view of the main waiting room of the Northern Pacific's Livingston station. The photograph was taken from the stairs up to the railroad offices.

on a large waiting room, with a ticket office, under a high ornamental ceiling. Off the waiting room were other spaces for travelers: a combination of women's rest, reclining, or dressing rooms by the toilet facilities; men's smoking room; barbershop; boot-black stands; and dining room or café. Above the ground floor, on second and sometimes third floors, were offices for administration of railroad operations, properties, and finances. Some stations had separate satellite buildings for baggage, express, or food service. The Northern Pacific station in Livingston, for example, had a baggage and express building to the west and a restaurant ("beanery") to the east. An ornately decorated roofed colonnade linked the three buildings.

For some large stations, the most visually striking aspect was the tower. Rising to one hundred or more feet, it might have been for decades the highest structure in a city. Some towers had clock faces on all four sides (Milwaukee in Butte, GN in Great Falls and Helena). The first railroad across Montana, the NP, had urban stations without towers in Billings, Butte, and Missoula, although the depot in Helena had a cupola with clocks. The last of the three transcontinental lines, the Milwaukee Road, had towers on all three of its large urban terminals in Montana, in Butte, Great Falls, and Missoula. The Milwaukee building in Missoula has two towers, one tall and one short, with identical curved parapets.

The large railway stations were individually designed by architects. By the early twentieth century, some major railroads employed architects located in company departments responsible for engineering and structures. The two Great Falls stations were designed by architects employed by each railroad: Samuel Bartlett designed the GN station built in 1909–10, which features an octagonal tower, and J. A. Lindstrand designed the Milwaukee station built in 1915.[5] Other railroads commissioned architectural firms for major projects. In the early twentieth century, the Northern Pacific hired the firm of Charles Reed and Allen Stem, of St. Paul, to design many of the stations along its main line, including those at Bismarck, North Dakota, Livingston and Missoula in Montana, and stations shared with the Great Northern in Seattle and Tacoma, Washington.[6] While all five of these stations survive, only King Street Station in Seattle remains in railway use.

Urban stations had two arrangements in relation to the tracks. The most common in Montana was the "through or side" layout,

Ron V. Nixon, photographer, MOR RVN 22269

The Milwaukee Road station at Missoula. A long, eastbound *Olympian Hiawatha* is slowing for its stop on June 19, 1958. Just to the right of the electric locomotive is the car scale and scale house for weighing freight cars loaded in Missoula.

Photographer unknown, MHS, PAc 74-104.226n

The Great Northern passenger station at Helena, here viewed from the south, was a stub station, and all tracks lay on the north side of the building. The GN removed the massive tower after it was badly damaged in an October 1935 earthquake. Also in the photo, left to right, are the Algeria Shrine (completed in 1921), buildings of Carroll College, and the warehouse of the State Nursery & Seed Co. (identified by large letters on the roof). The Helena branch bank of the U.S. Federal Reserve now occupies the site of the former station.

with the station on one side of through tracks extending in both directions. There trains stopped and then resumed travel without changing direction. A few stub (dead-end) tracks served for parked railcars or for trains originating or terminating at the station. But in the "head or stub station" plan, all tracks ended at the depot building, and thus all trains had to reverse direction upon departure, either backing into or out of the station.[7] These required more complicated operations—the reversal of all through trains—but allowed for a station to be closer to the dense central part of the city than a through station. The stations of the Milwaukee Road in Butte and the Great Northern at Helena were of the stub arrangement, with all tracks leading away from the city center.

In August 1916, as the Milwaukee Road anticipated completion of its passenger station in Butte, an article in the *Butte Miner* detailed aspects of the new building. Located on the west side of South Montana Street, the façade of the main portion—the "head house"—faced eastward onto a half-circular drive connected to the street. The head house included a ninety-five-foot-tall tower with clock faces six and one-half feet in diameter. Inside on the ground floor were waiting rooms, restrooms, and a lunch room and kitchen, with company offices on the second floor. The back portion—the

The Milwaukee Road passenger depot in Butte hosted an event covered in nationwide news in November 1926. Inability to pay debts had forced the Chicago, Milwaukee & St. Paul Railway into receivership in 1925. A crucial part of the financial reorganization process was the formal sale of the railway by the trustees to the new owners. This public sale took place in Butte, near the midpoint of the Puget Sound extension, in the depot's entry vestibule. Nationally prominent merchant bankers, business lawyers, bankruptcy administrators, and company officials rode the train to Butte to attend. This photograph was apparently taken just after the depot's completion because the ground in the foreground is bare dirt.

Photographer unknown, MHS, PAc 2013-50.1460

baggage and express wing—also included facilities for employees: lodging and a clubroom and toilet facilities for trainmen. One hundred and sixty tons of structural steel went into the building's frame and the narrow shed roofs over each of three platforms between the six stub tracks. The exterior was pressed brick.[8] The building served the Milwaukee Road for forty years, until 1957. At that time, it was replaced by a much smaller depot to the south on the main line, where the only remaining pair of passenger trains stopped without backing in or out. The grand 1917 structure now houses a television station on the ground floor and a consulting firm on the second floor. There, in the former railroad offices, some of the frosted glass panels in wooden doors still carry the Milwaukee's tilted rectangle emblem and lettering for offices of the superintendent and chief dispatcher.[9]

Most stations in towns and cities were operated by just one railway. Thus, many towns and cities had as many stations as railroads. In Montana, this was true of Missoula, Great Falls, and Helena, all served by two railroads each with its own station. In some cases,

Photographer(s) unknown, MHS, PAc 83-33.8 (top), PAc 83-33.9 (bottom)

Passenger trains of three railroads served the Billings train station, built in 1909: Northern Pacific, Burlington Route, and Great Northern. As evident in these two views, the local use of the name varied. In the street-side view, it is "Union Depot." The near building housed the lunch room and newsstand. On the trackside view, with express and baggage rooms nearest, it is called "Union Station."

however, two or more railways, even those competing on major routes, shared the use of a single station, a "union station." The main justification was to share costs, reducing expenditures for each partner, first for land acquisition and construction and then for operations and maintenance through subsequent decades. Some were officially designated or commonly named Union Station, while others were informally identified with the dominant railroad using the facility. In Butte, the Union Pacific was a minor partner with the Northern Pacific at the station on Front Street that was normally called the Northern Pacific station. The depot in Billings, on the NP main line, was completed in 1909 and called Union Station or Union Depot. It was the only depot in Montana to be served by trains of the three railroads: Northern Pacific, Burlington Route, and Great Northern. In 1916, it was the busiest single station in Montana, visited by twenty trains per day, including two jointly operated by the NP-Burlington and two by the GN-Burlington.[10]

Stations in Montana's Cities

In 1910, there were six cities in Montana with a population of over ten thousand, up from half that number a decade earlier. For the next three decades, and next three U.S. censuses—through 1940—these same six remained the only cities in Montana with over ten thousand residents. Four were along the mining-metallurgical axis of Butte, Anaconda, Helena, and Great Falls. The other two were Missoula and Billings. The largest railroad stations in Montana were concentrated in five of these cities. Only Anaconda, served by just one short-line railroad without through traffic, did not have a large station.

Each of the other large Montana cities was served by main lines of two or three major railroads. Their architecturally distinctive buildings not only housed railway services, but were also visually prominent evidence of railway utility and influence. In these five cities, there were ten large railroad stations, all built in the sixteen years between 1901 (NP station in Missoula) and 1917 (Milwaukee depot in Butte). Regularly scheduled passenger trains stopped at these stations for spans of time ranging from nearly four to almost eight decades. Rail passenger service to Montana cities ended during a quarter century—from 1955, when the Milwaukee ended service to Great Falls, to 1979, when Amtrak ended service through

Missoula, Butte, and Billings. Remarkably, all but one of the buildings, the GN station in Helena (demolished in 1989), survives into the twenty-first century in alternate uses. The former stations now house functions and offices for non-railroad businesses and organizations, a television station, and spaces for food, drink, and entertainment.

Multistory station buildings were also located in smaller cities and towns, where railroads based administrative and operating functions. Railroads divided their systems into geographical operating units called "divisions." In the early twentieth century, a division usually consisted of three hundred to six hundred miles of main line and connected branches. The number of employees and range of functions at division headquarters required large stations. As with larger urban terminals, the ground floor of division headquarters housed the usual passenger and express services. The second and third floors had offices and workrooms for the employees who oversaw the division's train operations and the engineering and maintenance of properties. The communications to dozens of stations within the division and to railroad offices beyond were the responsibility of the "relay office." A writer on railways described the relay offices, which included teletype printers, on the Santa Fe Railway in the 1940s: "Relay telegraph offices . . . are staffed by a manager or a wire chief, a night wire chief, a late night wire chief, telegraphers, telegrapher-printer clerks, printer clerks, messengers, and apprentices."[11]

Outside the most populous cities of Montana, there were five large multistory stations with division headquarters. The first and last of these were both built on the Great Northern. The first was at Kalispell, built in 1899. Just five years later, in 1904, the GN completed a new section of main line that relegated the rails through Kalispell to a branch line. The railway then created Whitefish on the new main line for an operating base and division offices and, in 1927, constructed a large station there, which also served tourist traffic for Glacier National Park. In some places, a building separate from the depot housed the division offices, as was the case in Havre on the GN and Miles City on the Milwaukee.

The offices of division headquarters had dozens of employees. In the Livingston offices, in 1916, these included regional and division superintendents, civil engineers, and train dispatchers, all supported by many clerks, stenographers, and telegraphers. The

In this May 13, 1942, photograph, Great Northern train No. 244 idles at the Kalispell station before the first of four daily northbound runs on the fifteen-mile branch to the main line at Columbia Falls to connect with transcontinental trains. The station was built in the 1890s to house main line division headquarters, but the completion of a new main line west of Columbia Falls through Whitefish relegated the original route through Kalispell to a branch line. For nearly seventy years, the Great Northern provided Kalispell with main line connections, using a sequence of steam trains, a self-propelled rail car, and finally a "bruck," a motor bus with a large baggage-freight compartment.

(top) Ron V. Nixon, photographer, MOR RVN 11765
(bottom) "Marble Photo" photograph, MHS, PAc 2013-50.1261

Built in 1927, the Great Northern Railway station at Whitefish, the largest town close to Glacier National Park, combined several functions, including serving as the division headquarters.

Ron V. Nixon, photographer, MOR RVN 01491

Ron Nixon took this self-portrait in August 1935 at age twenty-four while working as an operator in the telegraph relay office of the Northern Pacific division headquarters in Fargo, North Dakota. At this time, he already had ten years of experience in railroad telegraph work.

station served passengers, including those transferring between trains on the main line and Yellowstone Park branch line. On the ground floor of the main building and in the two satellite buildings, employees worked in ticket sales, baggage handling, express (the west building), and the "NP Lunch Room" (the east building), which still houses a café.[12]

Large urban stations were often located just beyond the edge of a central business district, where land was available within walking distance. Such was the case in Miles City, where the Northern Pacific located its track and station just south of the young town that grew up next to Fort Keogh. In some places in Montana, however, railroads established their stations more than one mile from the city center. This was true in the relatively rare cases where the town or city was established, platted, and developed before the arrival of the rail line, as in Helena, Butte, and Bozeman.

When the railway civil engineers considered the location and alignment of a rail line, they often selected a route on or beyond the edge of an existing town for two reasons. First, the railways needed enough undeveloped land for their facilities—station lots, sidings, switchyard, and locomotive facilities—as well as industrial lots next to the tracks for businesses reliant on shipping by rail. Open land on the edge of town was both available and less expensive to acquire. The other reason was to meet the engineering constraints of railway main lines, minimizing curvature and gradient that significantly reduced the pulling power of locomotives. Track as straight and close to level as possible was the priority.[13] Butte and Helena began as mining towns on hillsides above valley floors. Though less evident, Bozeman, a farm town nearly two decades old when the railroad reached it, is on a sloping valley floor. Main Street is almost fifty feet higher in elevation than the alignment the Northern Pacific selected on the northeast edge of town.

Locating the rail line away from an established community had two main consequences. The obvious one is that the railway passenger and freight stations were a fair walking distance from the business district and most residential areas. Where streetcar lines were created in towns like this, one of the first priorities was a line linking downtown and the railway station. Such was the case in Helena, Butte, and Bozeman.

The other consequence was the development of a secondary business district around the railway station that was a mile or more from the older downtown. Enterprises especially appropriate for

Photographer unknown, Gallatin History Museum, Bozeman, P5867-1

Attended by conductor Elmer Dinsmore, the Bozeman Street Railway car waiting by the Northern Pacific passenger station on Front Street in the mid-1910s is an example of urban transit meeting intercity transportation. The 2.6-mile Bozeman Street Railway linked the NP station with downtown, a mile to the southwest, and Montana State College, another mile from downtown. The street railway ended operations in 1921.

Photographer unknown, Yellowstone Gateway Museum, Livingston, 2006.044.6860

The central building of the Northern Pacific Railway station and division headquarters at Livingston housed many of the station functions on the ground floor and railroad offices above. The west satellite building, on the right, housed express, and a café operated in the east building. A roofed colonnade linked the three structures.

travelers and railroad workers established businesses close to the passenger stations. The most common were hotels, restaurants, saloons, and retail stores.

Butte

The first rail line reached Butte from Utah and Idaho in 1881. The Union Pacific established its terminal—switchyard, passenger station, freight house, and locomotive roundhouse—a full mile south of and 250 feet in elevation below the uptown business district that developed in the 1870s. The Northern Pacific, which first reached Butte from the east in 1890, shared the terminal properties with the UP, and it soon became the dominant partner. Around the railway terminal developed the satellite settlement called South Butte, initially with undeveloped land separating it from uptown Butte. On the south edge was Front Street, a name commonly used in many towns for the street next to and parallel to the tracks. Differently oriented street alignments—the conventional north-south and east-west grid of uptown Butte and the streets parallel and perpendicular to the tracks of South Butte—grew toward each other in the 1890s, already linked by streetcars. South Butte was for decades a railway community, meeting the residential and retail needs of rail workers and providing lodging, food, and entertainment to travelers. Because of the distance between the station and the uptown business district, the NP and UP each operated a "city ticket office" located uptown. In 1917, these were on opposite sides of Main Street at the busy intersection with Park Street.[14]

The passenger station on Front Street went through two physical incarnations and several names. In the 1890s, it was the "M. U. station" or "Montana Union station," after the name of the local railway jointly operated by the UP and NP. By the turn of the century, the NP acquired control of the property, and thus its name became the popular designation for the depot. Because of Butte's prosperity and population, the Northern Pacific operated its premier train between St. Paul and Puget Sound—the *North Coast Limited*—through Butte, instead of on the original main line through Helena.

Gamblers at one of the businesses next to the Northern Pacific station contributed to keeping one man in Butte. Burton K. Wheeler recalled: "On Sunday morning October 15, 1905, I stepped off a train at the Northern Pacific depot in Butte, Montana, and shivered. A sudden snowstorm had whipped out of the mountains and in my light summer suit and straw hat the air was bitter cold." After finishing law school at the University of Michigan, Wheeler traveled through many western states looking for work as a lawyer.

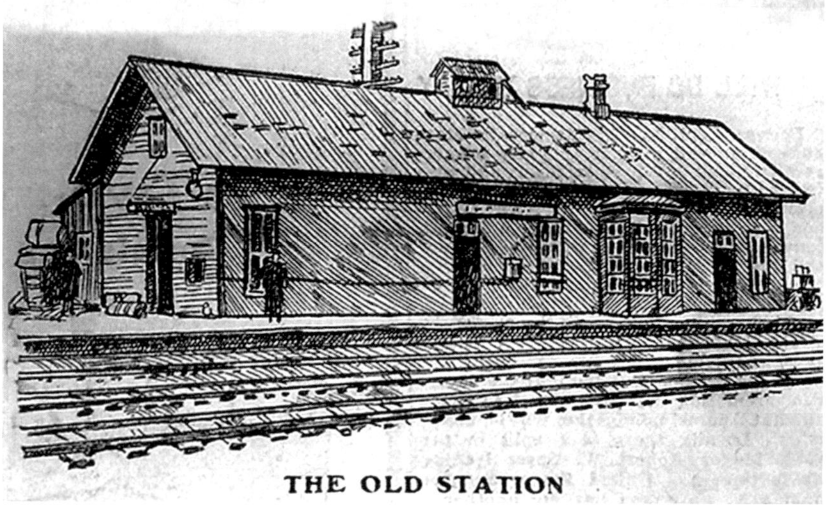

Anaconda (Mont.) Standard, September 11, 1906, Butte–Silver Bow Public Archives

Shared by the Northern Pacific and Union Pacific, this unremarkable building at the base of Butte Hill was the busiest station for a city of over fifty thousand residents as well as the station where the NP's premier *North Coast Limited* stopped on its transcontinental run. The *Anaconda Standard* published this illustration when the opening of the large new joint depot ended use of "the old station" in 1906.

After most of a week in Butte, he gave up on finding promising prospects there and decided to travel to Spokane. Approaching the NP station, Wheeler saw "there was a little yellow saloon" at the corner of Nevada Avenue and Front Street, where two men—one called Gladney—first engaged him in conversation and then persuaded him to join a poker game. He agreed, got into high-stakes betting, and "since I am by nature a plunger I decided to go for broke." He lost over two hundred dollars and then realized he'd been set up. He confronted the men and recovered less than one quarter of the loss. Without enough money to resume a full travel itinerary, he decided to "give Butte a try." Wheeler's law practice quickly flourished, he established his home in Butte, and he entered politics. Wheeler recalled decades later: "Long before [1910], I would have thanked Gladney for stranding me in Butte. I liked it."[15] Wheeler subsequently served as a state legislator and then U.S. district attorney for Montana, based in Butte. Seventeen years after the memorable poker game he was elected U.S. senator.

The railway station in B. K. Wheeler's story of 1905 was not the two-story brick station that survives today at the base of Butte hill. In 1905, the passenger station of the NP and UP in Butte was a

Photographer unknown, MHS, PAc 2013-50.1146

"Butte's New Passenger Depot" replaced the small building in the previous illustration. The main building opened on September 10, 1906, with final work on the buildings and track near completion. Many local and transcontinental trains of the Northern Pacific and Union Pacific trains on the route to Pocatello and Salt Lake City originated, terminated, or stopped here. The near (west) satellite building, with the ten shiny milk cans stacked by the wall and the mailbox on the nearest corner, housed baggage and express functions, with rooms for Union Pacific personnel. The far building was used for express and a restaurant—in railroaders' slang, a "beanery." The first train out of the station was a special carrying about one hundred local members of the Elks organization to the state meeting in Billings. The Boston & Montana Mining Company band played for the occasion.

narrow, one-story wooden building, much smaller than would seem adequate for the busiest depot in a city of about fifty thousand. The *Anaconda Standard* described it in 1906, at the end of its use:

> It was dark and dingy and dirty and would have disgraced the smallest branch line on the entire system. And the queer part of it was that passengers from three great railroads, the Northern Pacific, the Burlington [a St. Louis–Seattle train operated west of Billings by the NP] and the Oregon Short Line [UP], got off the cars every day in the year and they did not see anything queer about the building; it was just what they expected for a rough and ready mining town like Butte, where their idea of the people was that they were never particular.[16]

A citizen committee persuaded the Northern Pacific and Union Pacific to build a new station, which went into service on September 10, 1906. An attempt to build a union station, for all the trains serving the city, failed when the Great Northern refused to join the effort.[17]

The Northern Pacific–Union Pacific station hosted scheduled trains, special trains for organizations, and a seasonal "fishing train." Most of the way to the Idaho border, the Union Pacific line followed rivers—all tributaries of the Jefferson River: the Big Hole and the Beaverhead and its tributary, Red Rock Creek. During the summer of 1916, the UP's "Sunday Fishing Train" left Butte at 7:20 A.M., twenty minutes behind the scheduled day train to Salt Lake City. As it headed south, the crew stopped the train at the request of the anglers. The train went as far south as Armstead, eighty-nine miles from Butte, where it turned and awaited its return trip north. Stopping when flagged by anglers, it was scheduled to arrive back in Butte at 10:05 P.M.[18] The Great Northern also operated a fishing train southeast from Great Falls on the branch line to Neihart, dropping people at spots along Belt Creek in the Little Belt Mountains.

John K. Hutchens in Missoula

John K. Hutchens arrived in Missoula in July 1917, at the age of eleven, when his father became the editor and publisher of the city's morning and evening newspapers, issued by the same enterprise. In his memoir *One Man's Montana,* Hutchens included stories of

The eastbound *North Coast Limited*, with its name and NP's monad on the drumhead sign on the railing of the observation car, is stopped for passengers, mail, and change of crews and locomotives at the Northern Pacific passenger station at Missoula. One of the business cars on the stub tracks, on the right, is likely for the use of railway officials. The other car may also be for railway use or belong to a wealthy individual.

R. H. McKay, photographer, MHS, PAc 2013-50.1218

trains on the Northern Pacific and Milwaukee Road into and out of Missoula. Episodes included his initial arrival on NP's premier *North Coast Limited* and riding a year later to Deer Lodge with his father to attend the public funeral of Montana pioneer Granville Stuart. On the verge of adulthood, he and a friend rode "the Butte *Stub*—a local train, as distances went in Montana"—for a weekend experience in Butte appropriate for a young man who, in the words of an older reporter, "has reached a certain age." Young Hutchens worked at the newspaper his father edited and particularly admired one reporter who covered sports and the locally significant "Forestry service and railroad news."[19]

Railway stations were gateways for hopes and dreams, perhaps passed through again after either success or failure. The gathering of interested people at some departures and returns made them unofficial public events. Hutchens related a story from the early 1920s of Eddie Bennett, "a Missoula boy [who] displayed unmistakable signs of more than ordinary talent as a second baseman." With the connections and encouragement of a Missoula man Hutchens calls "Postcard Smith," Bennett went to the Texas training camp of the New York Giants to try out for the team. He departed one late winter morning. "At the station Postcard made a speech, gave the boy some last-minute advice and a new pair of spiked shoes." A short time in Texas proved that the talent that stood out in Montana did not rate there. Bennett had to return to Missoula.

> So, on Saturday, we were all at the station. Eddie climbed off the train, with his cardboard suitcase and a Texas training camp tan, but looking somehow pale beneath that tan, and more than a few months older.
>
> The boy saw the crowd and was startled. Then he looked at Postcard, who seemed suddenly aged and beaten, a fallen sage.

Bennett reassured Postcard that his time in Texas was not a total loss, and neither he nor Postcard should feel defeated. The crowd soon cheered "the kid who had gone to the far places, got one hit off the great Art Nehf, robbed Frank Frisch of a hit, and was not afraid to come home."[20]

Splendid Façades

Unlike many small-town stations that appeared in historical photographs primarily as backdrops for people, larger urban stations were often the primary subject in photos. With their impressive size, complicated rooflines, and exterior ornamentation, urban stations were among the most important buildings in major towns and cities. Thus, these stations appeared, along with the largest hotels, office buildings, churches, and schools, as favorite subjects in visual documentation of a city's prosperity, growth, and claims to regional or even national prominence.

The angle of view in photographs is often from the street side, as seen by the residents of the city and those who worked in the neighboring business districts. This façade was the one the architect intended for the public to admire and photographers to record. In contrast, views from the railway side were often cluttered with tracks, trains, parked railcars, baggage trucks loaded with mail and express, platform sheds, or auxiliary buildings.

Photographer unknown, MHS, PAc 2007.12.1

The staff of Northern Pacific's city office in Helena pose for a photograph on July 29, 1890. The office was located on Main Street (now the Last Chance Gulch pedestrian mall) in the southern part of Helena's business district. There, staff provided passenger tickets, express service, and arranged freight shipments, saving customers a trip to the railroad's passenger station or freight house, both one and a half miles away on the east edge of the city. The poster in the left display window shows a steamship. The NP offered connections to ocean travel and shipping.

Street-side view of the Northern Pacific passenger station in Missoula

Photographer(s) unknown, MHS, (top) PAc 2013-50.1220, (bottom) PAc 83.33.2

The Butte, Anaconda & Pacific depot on the north side of Anaconda. The Montana Union Railway, which served Anaconda before the construction of the BA&P, built this station. In 1898, five years after the BA&P reached Anaconda, it leased all the Montana Union properties. The electric locomotive on the right edge of the photograph places this photograph in 1913 or later. The building survives, and it now houses a hardware and building supplies store.

Photographer(s) unknown, MHS, (top) PAc 83.33.31, (bottom) PAc 83.33.33

These two photos are of the Northern Pacific stations and division headquarters at Glendive. The older photograph (before 1922) shows the wood-frame building and the adjoining fenced park, a feature of some larger stations. The roundhouse is in the right background above the boxcar. You can see the smoke vents on the roundhouse roof that expelled smoke from locomotives in the building. The lower photograph shows the new depot built in 1922 with a large crowd gathered.

Street-side view of the Northern Pacific passenger station at Helena, on the east edge of the city. The left (west) wing houses the baggage room and the right (east) wing the lunch room.

Both photos, courtesy of David Hull

NOR. PAC. LUNCH ROOM
UNION DEPOT HELENA MONT
Estella
This is not the one I promised, Keep your Eye open for another
F. C. R.
3/23/07.

The term "Union Depot" for the Northern Pacific station in Helena implies that trains of more than one railroad stopped at the station. The other railroad in Helena, the Great Northern, had its own station closer to the downtown. The unnamed other railroad at the NP depot may be the Burlington Route, which jointly operated with the NP a pair of St. Louis–Seattle passenger trains through Helena and southern Montana.

CHAPTER 5

Railroad Views

THE RAILROAD right-of-way was a linear property where people, both on the ground and on trains, saw the world of their counterparts, respectively, moving and stationary. Those on the ground saw passing trains both familiar and unusual. Those on the trains saw, of course, the larger landscape but also the literally narrow world of railway work and rail-centered life within the right-of-way just outside the car windows. The railroad right-of-way was centered on the main track, normally extending on each side between seventy-five and two hundred feet. The continuous linear features included the main track, with passing sidings and spur tracks, the telegraph-telephone pole line, and wire fences to keep livestock off the railroad property.

When railroads dominated land transport, they carried a wide variety of passengers, including individuals and groups of great interest to people living along the line. Those traveling in special trains received extra attention: circuses, carnivals, theater troupes, groups traveling to conventions and picnics, troops going to training camp and embarkation for overseas service, and politicians.

Presidents on Trains in Montana

One select group who rode trains that regularly brought hundreds or even thousands to trackside were politicians, in office or seeking election, especially as president of the United States. During the decades of regular and prolonged campaigning by rail—the 1890s into the 1950s—people in towns and small cities throughout the United States saw more presidents, and candidates seeking that office, than in the time before, when few candidates left their home town to campaign, or after, when most relied on travel by airplane to major cities. Historian Gil Troy considered the half century starting in the 1890s:

> In retrospect, the period from 1896 to 1944 would become a Golden Age of campaigning. As actors, the nominees were somewhat calculating and artificial, but on the whole appeared intimate and authentic. The "Campaign Special," rumbling through America morning, noon, and night, displayed the nominees in unguarded moments, be it Charles Hughes running to catch his own campaign train, or Al Smith greeting early risers in his P.J.'s.[1]

During that time, major party candidates for president and vice president had the money to charter special campaign trains that carried the candidates, their family, campaign staff, reporters, and local political figures who joined the entourage for short segments. In some cases, presidents in office traveled extensively in the United States in the year before the next election. Thus, they got out to see

Library of Congress, LC-DIG-stereo-1s02083

A stereo-card view of the special train that carried President Theodore Roosevelt on a two-month trip through the Midwest and West during the spring of 1903. Roosevelt spent over two weeks in Yellowstone National Park. The Northern Pacific had not completed its new terminal at Gardiner, so the presidential train used the old terminal at Cinnabar, three miles to the north, where it was photographed on the wye, a Y-shaped arrangement of tracks for turning trains. The six-car train consisted of a baggage car, a club car, a diner, two sleeping cars—for the press, telegraphers, Secret Service, White House staff, and presidential guests—and at the end, the private car, "Elysian," for the president.

Photographer unknown, Gallatin History Museum, Bozeman, PA 16063-11

President William Howard Taft speaks from a temporary platform, with the roof of Northern Pacific's passenger station at Bozeman behind him, on October 19, 1911. The *Bozeman Chronicle* reported that between three thousand and four thousand people attended. Taft was touring the United States to promote several programs, including proposed rural post office savings banks, and probably also in preparation to run for reelection a year later.

the nation, to meet and be seen by thousands of people, to promote causes important to them, and in some cases, without stating it, to prepare for next year's contest. In this way, Theodore Roosevelt in 1903, William Howard Taft in 1911, Woodrow Wilson in 1919, and Warren Harding in 1923 all visited Montana.

At least eight presidents and two candidates for president rode trains in Montana.[2] The first president to do so made no official public appearances. In 1883, Chester Arthur visited Yellowstone National Park, arriving from the south through Wyoming and departing across the northern boundary, then riding a special train on the Northern Pacific from Cinnabar north through Livingston, and then eastward.[3]

Just three years after statehood brought Montanans the right to vote in national elections, the first presidential candidate campaigned in Montana. In August 1892, James Weaver, of the Peoples' Party (better known as the Populists), included Montana in his tour of the West. Traveling on regularly scheduled trains, he and his small party rode into Helena from the west on a Northern Pacific local train from the main line junction of Garrison. At NP's Helena passenger station, more than a mile northeast of downtown,

Weaver and his party were greeted by about one hundred people, the city band, and a salute from the local artillery battery. From the station, two chartered streetcars headed downtown, the first carrying the city band and the second the visitors and reception committee. The *Helena Independent,* a paper with Democratic affiliation, generally approved of Weaver and his speech at the city auditorium but noted (in a familiar refrain about third-party candidates) that "a vote for Weaver is a vote wasted"—it would only help the Republican incumbent, Benjamin Harrison. "GEN. WEAVER is the first presidential candidate who has ever visited the state, and we appreciate the compliment. But Miss Montana can only be a sister to him; her heart is a democrat."[4] Weaver and the Populists won four states in the electoral college and, as the *Helena Independent* predicted, threw Montana to Harrison, who lost the election to Grover Cleveland.

Major party politicians campaigning by special train often left the train to speak, especially in cities and large towns. At large cities, the candidate orated at venues for many hundreds or even thousands of people, in large public buildings or outdoors. In smaller places, they spoke on temporary wooden platforms—which sometimes collapsed under pressure from too many people—erected close to the train.

But in many towns, the politicians did not leave the train. Instead, during a stop that might last only five to ten minutes—a "whistle stop"—they spoke briefly from the brass-railed back platform of the observation car at the end of the train. This practice began in 1896, with the campaign of William Jennings Bryan, the presidential nominee of both the Democratic and Populist parties, who was inspired to take his campaign on the road by the example of James Weaver four years earlier. Bryan had more resources than Weaver, and he campaigned from a sequence of special trains through the Midwest, Northeast, and border South. (Bryan didn't campaign in the West or deep South, where he knew he already had strong support.) The public repeatedly surrounded his train, making it difficult to get off, and so, according to Gil Troy, Bryan "simply spoke from the rear platform of the last car, and a campaign tradition was born."[5]

Bryan himself described the new approach in more detail in his memoir of the 1896 campaign, published that year, presenting it as advice to others who would campaign by rail:

> As we learn by experience, my experience may be of value to those who may hereafter be engaged in a similar campaign. I soon found that it was necessary to stand upon the rear platform of the last car in order to avoid danger to those who crowded about the train. I also found that it was much easier to speak from the platform of the car than to go to a stand, no matter how close. . . . Speaking from the car also avoided the falling of platforms, a form of danger which, all through the campaign, I feared more than I feared breaking down from overwork.[6]

Thus the familiar pose of a candidate on a train, standing with family and staff at the brass railing of the observation car platform, became for decades a standard image of electoral politics.

Photographer unknown, MOR x 85.2.541

President Franklin Roosevelt prepares to orate from his special train on the Great Northern main line in northern Montana. Sitting on the railing, at the right side of the platform of the observation car, is Montana's senior U.S. senator, Burton K. Wheeler. In August 1934, FDR headed eastward across the northwestern United States, visiting three large dams being built as part of New Deal public works: Bonneville Dam on the lower Columbia River, Grand Coulee on the middle Columbia, and Fort Peck on the Missouri River in northeastern Montana. Roosevelt left the train at Glasgow to go by automobile to Fort Peck on August 6.

After his defeat in 1896, W. J. Bryan intended to run again for president in 1900, and he traveled in the intervening years with that intent. In mid-August 1897, he came to Montana, arriving in Butte from Utah and Idaho. Traveling as a private citizen by scheduled Union Pacific train, his arrival in Butte and at other stops was as rapturously greeted as if he were formally campaigning. Charles H. Eggleston, of the *Anaconda Standard,* witnessed the crowds greeting Bryan in Butte, and the next day the newspaper published a poem Eggleston wrote comparing the celebration of Bryan's arrival to a Roman triumph, Napoleon's return from exile on Elba, and Queen Victoria's diamond jubilee. Eggleston concluded the poem with:

> Of the earth's great celebrations 'twas the champion
> heavyweight,
> 'Tis the champion forever and a day, I calculate,
> For it knocked out all its rivals, and, undaunted, resolute,
> Punched creation's solar plexus—
> When Bryan came to Butte.[7]

In 1900, the first member of a presidential ticket to campaign from a special train in Montana was Theodore Roosevelt, vice presidential candidate under William McKinley. (Roosevelt became president just one year later, after the assassination of McKinley.) The visibility he got from his train is evident in the list of places where the train stopped, however briefly. Roosevelt's train on the Northern Pacific main line entered Montana from North Dakota midday on September 16 and stopped at Glendive, Miles City, Forsyth, Billings (overnight), Columbus, Big Timber, Livingston, Bozeman, Manhattan, Logan, Townsend, and Winston before reaching Helena (overnight). It then went south on the Great Northern with stops at Clancy, Boulder, Basin, and Butte (overnight). Then, after three days in Montana, on the nineteenth, the train headed south on the Union Pacific, stopping at Dillon and Lima before entering Idaho.[8]

For the famous, the public went to a town's station, even when the train didn't stop. In the late summer of 1919, Woodrow Wilson toured the nation, trying to persuade the public and, through them, U.S. senators to ratify the Treaty of Versailles and approve United States' membership in the League of Nations. The special train carrying Wilson and his party crossed southern Montana in

President Harry S. Truman talks to the crowd from the rear platform of a special train backed onto the Great Northern station tracks in Helena on May 12, 1950. U.S. representative (and after 1952, U.S. senator) Mike Mansfield stands behind the doorway. The car is U.S. Car No. 1, the Pullman observation car named "Ferdinand Magellan," specially modified and armored in 1943 for presidential travel. Note the presidential seal incorporated into the platform railing. The B&O SPECIAL signs indicate that the Baltimore & Ohio Railroad operated the train for both the first stage of the trip from Washington, D.C. to the Midwest and the last leg back to D.C.

Photographer unknown, MHS, PAc 81-71.2

mid-September. On the eleventh, after a stop in Billings, the train headed west toward Wilson's next public appearance, in Helena. Although it did not pause in Bozeman, townspeople still went to trackside to see the train and perhaps catch a glimpse of the president. The editor of the *Bozeman Chronicle* began the next day's editorial: "To those citizens of Bozeman who lined up along the railroad track yesterday afternoon and got a good view of President Wilson as the long train slowly swept by." He noted that Wilson, as seen through the windows of the last car, was of unremarkable appearance.[9] Just over two weeks later, on the twenty-sixth, in eastern Colorado, the stress of the western tour broke Wilson's health, and his train raced back to Washington, D.C.

Library of Congress, LC-USZ62-102876

This stereo-card view shows President Warren G. Harding in the engineer's seat of a Milwaukee Road electric passenger locomotive, at Falcon, Idaho, ten miles west of the crest of the Bitterroot Mountains, on July 2, 1923. Harding briefly "drove" the locomotive under the close watch of the engineer. Since Harding died in California during the last part of the long trip (all the way to Alaska), this card became one way of remembering a popular president, before emergence of the administration's scandals after his death.

Four years later, President Warren G. Harding traveled through Montana on his transcontinental trip to the Pacific coast and briefly rode in an electric locomotive. In July 1923, a late change in the itinerary of his special train, traveling west across Montana, resulted in an unusual change of power at a small junction community east of Butte. At Sappington, the main lines of the Northern Pacific and Milwaukee crossed at the same level on the south side of the Jefferson River, and an interchange track allowed trains to transfer from one railroad to the other. Just about midnight at the end of July 1, an NP steam locomotive pulled Harding's train into Sappington. There, the Milwaukee Road had an electric locomotive waiting to pull the train through Butte, sixty miles west, and farther across western Montana. After crossing the crest of the Bitterroot Mountains into Idaho, Harding rode in the engine and held the controller, under the close watch of the engineer. Harding "declared his experience to be one of the finest thrills he has had in many a day."[10] For the Milwaukee, proud of its long main line electrification that was less than a decade old, this was valuable publicity. A photographer for the Milwaukee captured Harding aboard the engine, in the engineer's position. One month later on this trip, on

August 2, Harding died in California. Grieving citizens lined tracks, as another special train carried his body back across the country.

Trains for Troops, Silk, Agricultural Demonstration, and Game Day

Wartime brought increased train traffic to the nation's railways, including special trains for moving troops. In 1917 and 1918, young Dan Cushman, in Zurich on the Great Northern main line, saw the trains first gathering troops for training camp and then again for transport to embarkation for France: "How with ringing rails the troop trains rolled through Zurich! *Too-ot!* the steam whistle went, leaving echo in its wake and the sulphury smell of Sand Coulee coal. They were unlike any trains we'd ever seen."[11]

Westbound trains through Zurich picked up recruits at the major towns and junctions on the Hi-Line and took them to basic training at Camp (now Fort) Lewis, south of Tacoma. Cushman recalled: "On Sept. 21, a train of 14 cars started from Williston, loaded 133 in Bainville [junction for the branch to Plentywood and

W. T. Cheney, photographer, MHS, PAc 80-17.41

Troops march while their special train stops at Lima, on the Union Pacific, to change crews and locomotives during World War I. The station is the distant building with the diamond-shaped window in the gable end. At the far right is the facility for supplying coal to the tenders of steam locomotives.

Scobey], 110 from Glasgow, 90 from Malta and 76 from Chinook, a total of just about 500 when Havre was reached," with even more boarding in towns west of Havre. "The train ran without much schedule because there were celebrations all along the way." This train and others westbound were decorated; "the flags snapped on the engine while starry bunting streamed from the sides of coaches, patriotic remnants of farewell ceremonies along the line as successive communities in Minnesota, North Dakota and eastern Montana saw their contingents off to camp."[12]

Trains in the opposite direction carried the uniformed troops toward Atlantic coast ports:

> The eastbound trains were undecorated, filled and jam-filled with soldiers, khaki clad, graduates of Camp Lewis, Tacoma, Washington, heading for port of embarkation. Even when the trains passed through Zurich, the least of places, a clutch of wooden buildings fast receding into the emptiness of land and sky, young fellows leaned from the windows and waved to the girls on the platform (informed half an hour before by railroad telegraph) ankle-length dresses bright in the sun, "Yoo-hoo, rainbow!" and "I love my wife but oh you kid!" And from the windows a shower of picture postcards, free from the Y.M.C.A., or rolled pieces of paper, each with a soldier's name and Army mailing code, please write. All the girls collected soldiers' names and wrote to them. My sister and Agnes Sorenson might be the only girls standing in Zurich, hence to receive a harvest of cards.[13]

One of the most exciting sights for people in towns on railway main lines in the early decades of the twentieth century was the rapid passage of trains carrying bales of silk from East Asia to mills in the eastern United States. The fast runs crossed the West on transcontinental main lines linking Pacific coast seaports and eastern railway connections at Chicago and carried loads valued at over one million dollars. All three transcontinental railways across Montana ran silk trains, starting at the waterfront in Seattle.

> Due to the high value, high insurance costs, and interest on the [borrowed] money while in transit, speed was of the essence. The ships of the American Mail Line docked [in Seattle] at Piers 40 and 41 (now 90 and 91). The selected railroad had a train waiting on the wharf con-

sisting of eight to possibly fifteen express or baggage cars. These had been carefully checked over to be sure all was in readiness and all wheel bearings were perfect.[14]

Once loaded, the trains headed east, with the highest priority over nearly all other trains, and caught the attention of people in towns along the route.

Two residents of Tekoa in eastern Washington south of Spokane remembered silk trains passing eastward through their town on the Milwaukee Road's main line, which soared on a long, high steel trestle over the creek flats and the switchyard of the Union Pacific Railroad:

2505
$1000000. Silk Train
At. Avery. Idaho. Photo By Fish

MOR RVN 25830

A short "silk train" pauses at the Milwaukee Road division point of Avery, Idaho, in about 1915. Most of the silk crossing North America eastward from Pacific ports rode in trains made up of baggage-express cars. In this train, however, the bales of silk were transported in four insulated refrigerator cars designed to carry perishable produce and other foodstuffs. The silk from East Asia was bound for mills in the northeastern United States. A few years later, this switchyard would be under wires when Avery became the western end of the Milwaukee Road's electrification over the Rockies and Bitterroots.

> The whistle of an eastbound train sounded for a road crossing west of Tekoa. Soon the fast, ragged exhaust of the steam locomotive interrupted the slow chugging of the switch engine in the Union Pacific yards. Townspeople sensed the speed of the approaching train, paused in their activities, and looked toward the trestle. A passenger locomotive appeared on it, followed by express cars full of raw silk from the Orient bound for eastern mills. Worth nearly one million dollars, the cargo was insured against transportation risks at high hourly rates. Dozens of wheels set the bridge girders into roaring vibration. Whistling for the Washington Street crossing and the depot, the train passed through north Tekoa without slowing. Within one minute the train disappeared among the hills east of town and the crashing of freight car couplers in the switchyard was again noticeable.[15]

In the early twentieth century, in the United States and Canada, railroads and agricultural colleges cooperated to send trains carrying current teaching and research on farming and crops to farm towns. These "demonstration trains" included passenger cars equipped with exhibits and space for lectures by traveling faculty and freight cars displaying examples of current farm machinery and implements. The schedule of the train was published, so that farm families could plan a trip into town to see it. The agricultural department at Montana State College in Bozeman cooperated with the Northern Pacific to run the "Better Farming Special" for the first time in June 1910, and again in March 1911. On the train in 1911 were twenty-three administrators, faculty, and staff—including four women—from the college, among them both the president and head of the Experiment Station, as well as presenters on various aspects of farming and domestic science.[16] Across the international boundary, Wallace Stegner's family alternated between living most of the year in Eastend, Saskatchewan, on a Canadian Pacific Railway secondary line, and spending summers on a homestead to the south. In farming, they "used the methods and the machinery that were said to be right, and planted the crops and the varieties advised by rumor or the Better Farming Train."[17]

When large groups traveled to conventions and special events, they often rode on chartered trains. Large groups often required several trains (called "sections") running under a single authorized schedule. Such extras attracted attention in an era when people noted the unusual, and unscheduled, trains passing through their town. The front of locomotives of extra trains had a pair of white flags. In August 1892, four lodges of the Sons of St. George, a national fraternal group of English immigrants and descendants of immigrants, rode the Northern Pacific from Butte to Bozeman for a summer picnic. Three sections carried about 3,500 "Butteites." The "gaily decorated" first section with eleven cars arrived in Bozeman at 11:30 A.M. From the Bozeman train station, the visitors took "street cars, busses, hacks, and many carriages" to the Bogert Park "grove" for the day's activities. Trains were scheduled to depart for the return to Butte at 8:00, 9:00, and 10:30 P.M. The fare for the round-trip was two dollars.[18]

In Montana, for over a century perhaps the biggest sports event each year has been the annual football game, played since 1897, between the University of Montana in Missoula and Montana State University in Bozeman. Sports-oriented people along the tracks between Bozeman and Missoula knew to look for the special trains carrying fans. From 1926 to 1950, except during the war years of 1942–45, the game was played in Butte, centrally located on rail main lines between the two towns. Butte had a stadium with a larger capacity than either college campus, and it offered a better place for a full day of associated activities. The "Butte game" became an event of primary importance to college students, alumni, and sports fans around the state. Through this entire period, special trains for fans ran to Butte.

While just one rail main line linked Bozeman and Butte, that of the Northern Pacific, there were two nearly parallel main lines between Missoula and Butte, those of the NP and the Milwaukee Road. Each railroad had separate terminals in both cities. On game day in the first two years of the "Butte game," the NP ran one special train from Bozeman, and out of Missoula the NP and Milwaukee each operated a special train to their stations, located about four-fifths of a mile apart at the base of Butte hill. The Butte Electric Railway ran streetcars on frequent schedules from the stations to the stadium south of the hill.[19]

The 1937 version of the special from Bozeman was scheduled to leave there at 6:00 A.M. and reach Butte at 9:15. The passengers had time in uptown Butte to watch the parade and enjoy the festivities before going to the game at Clark Park stadium on the Flat. Allowing for more time in Butte after the game, the return train

Photographer(s) unknown, MSU, (top) 806, (bottom) 853

In the early twentieth century, railroads worked with land-grant agricultural colleges to operate demonstration trains that stopped throughout farming regions during times when farm work was slow. The railcars carried exhibits, lecturers, machinery, and animals. These two photos show details of demonstration trains operated by the Northern Pacific and Montana State College in Bozeman. The men standing in front of the baggage car with the banners are in Wibaux in 1910.

to Bozeman did not leave until 8:45 P.M. The rail fare for over six hours of travel in this eighteen-hour day was $1.95.[20] The Northern Pacific operated a special train from Bozeman to the Butte game each year through 1947 and from Missoula through the last Butte game in 1950. In 1951, the location of the game returned to alternating between the two college stadiums.[21]

On the Ground: Trains and Tracks in Daily Life

People certainly noticed the special trains through their town, but they also knew the schedules of daily trains and noted their appearance, both for practical reasons and as part of the familiar backdrop of daily life. Teresa Jordan grew up on a ranch north of Cheyenne, Wyoming, close to a Burlington Route main line linking Billings, Casper, Cheyenne, and Denver. She recalled the nighttime role of the Denver-Billings passenger trains in one era of her mother's life in the mid-1950s:

> Then, when I arrived [was born], I was not the easy, happy baby that Blade [her brother] had been. I was colicky; after my 2 A.M. feeding I would cry inconsolably for hours. She would walk me and walk me, and when she was so tired she couldn't walk anymore, she would set me back in my crib and close the door, go downstairs, and have a cup of coffee before she would go back to walk me some more.
>
> . . .
>
> The railroad ran a quarter mile in front of our house and a [passenger] train passed by every morning at three. There was no crossing—the tracks ran parallel to the road—but when a light shone in the kitchen, the engineer would sound his whistle.
>
> I think of my mother sitting at the table, drinking coffee and smoking cigarettes, fifty miles from town and two miles from a neighbor, alone in the center of the night, listening to that blue whistle blow.[22]

The railway was a well-used footpath particularly in towns and cities. It was especially useful when tracks cut a diagonal shortcut across rectangular grids of either city streets or section-line roads, the basis of rural travel a century ago. And when many roads were unimproved and seasonally muddy or dusty, the gravel and sand ballast and wooden crossties between the rails were an all-weather path. Poet Vachel Lindsay walked in 1912 from Illinois to Colorado, mostly on rail lines. He noted, "When I asked the way to Tipton [Missouri] the farmer wanted me to walk the railroad. People cannot see 'why the Sam Hill' anyone wants to walk the highway when the rails make a bee-line for the destination."[23] Lindsay addressed the issue noticed by many walkers of rail track—the spacing of the crossties—in the context of having wistfully contemplated entering politics: "Once I determined to be a candidate, I knew I would get

Photograph by the author

Burlington train No. 30 stopped in Worland, Wyoming, in the early evening of July 9, 1967, on its run from Billings to Denver. The single coach for passengers had no food service, so the train paused for forty minutes to allow the passengers to walk to dinner at a nearby restaurant, guided by the conductor. During the 1950s and into the 1960s, the Burlington's passenger trains between Denver and Billings passed through sparsely populated southeastern Wyoming during the night. The passage of an illuminated train was particularly noted by people in small towns and on ranches who were awake late at night or early in the morning. Writer Teresa Jordan's mother, sitting in the kitchen on a remote ranch with a sleepless baby, was grateful for the moment of connection to the larger world provided when an engineer offered brief greetings by locomotive horn.

the tramp-vote and the actor-vote. My platform was to be that railroad ties should be just close enough for men to walk on them in natural steps, neither mincing the stride nor widely stretching the legs."[24]

The View from the Cars

A century ago the typical main line railroad right-of-way was a busy place. It was filled with things that moved—primarily trains and work equipment, as well as people on trains, at stations, and on the ground—and things that didn't move—the fixed plant that included tracks on earthworks and bridges and the many buildings and structures necessary for operations and maintenance. It was a linear place encompassing travel, work, residence, and footpath.

Photographer unknown, MHS, PAc 99-45.1

The Northern Pacific interlocking tower (also called "signal tower") at the junction of Garrison, west of Helena. Through levers linked to steel wires and rods extending from the building to, respectively, signals and switches, workers on the windowed upper floor followed dispatcher's orders to enable the movement of trains through the junction. At Garrison, a single main line extended westward. To the east were two main lines across the Continental Divide: the original line through Helena and the later passenger route through Butte. This photograph was apparently taken just after completion of the building because there are no telegraph wires or poles to provide communication connections to the railway's network.

Ron V. Nixon, photographer, MOR RVN 11079

The Northern Pacific repair shops at Livingston, viewed from the north, in May 1933. This shops complex was the largest on the NP between Minnesota and western Washington. The long gable-roofed building is the "backshop," where workers—including machinists, blacksmiths, boilermakers, and pipefitters—did everything up to the complete rebuilding of locomotives. In the roundhouse, just to the left, with forty-four stalls, workers did engine inspections and light running repairs. The 176-foot-tall smokestack marks the location of the power plant between the backshop and roundhouse. The shops also had facilities for repairing freight cars and work equipment for track maintenance.

Ron V. Nixon, photographer, MOR RVN 08122

The interior of the backshop building at Livingston, in May 1933, with steam locomotives in various stages of repair work.

Robert H. Graham, photographer, MOR RVN 08842

A rail passenger's view of Drummond, with business buildings facing the railway across Front Street, on November 26, 1920. A passenger arriving at Drummond and needing to rent a horse or horse-pulled vehicle could easily see the painted LIVERY sign over a block away.

Ron V. Nixon, photographer, MOR RVN 10657

Before air-conditioning required sealed windows, passengers could lean out from the cars through windows that opened upward or, on certain scenic routes, from open-sided observation cars. Ron Nixon took this photograph from an open observation car at the end of a special train heading north along the Yellowstone River just north of Gardiner on June 17, 1940.

Passengers saw the buildings, structures, and workers of the railroad. They saw the stations in towns, of course, but also water tanks and coaling towers for the steam locomotives. They viewed the repetitive dip and rise of the telegraph wires, the flickering steel lattice of through truss bridges over rivers, and the isolated railway communities—telegraph office, section base, and water tank—seen only from trains. The passengers saw interlocking towers (or "signal towers"), the small but tall buildings in which workers on the second floor controlled the signals and switches at important junctions and crossings of main lines. These towers were rare in Montana but could be seen, for example, on the Northern Pacific at Garrison and just east of Belgrade. They noticed the flurry of activity at division points—at the station, roundhouse, and switchyard—where trains stopped for ten minutes or more for inspection, change of crews, and perhaps locomotives as well. Passengers also saw the large industrial complexes of the repair "shops," where hundreds of workers maintained and repaired locomotives and cars: Miles City and Deer Lodge on the Milwaukee, Livingston on the NP, and Great Falls on the Great Northern.

The crews that maintained and repaired the tracks and related structures were, after stations, perhaps the most common sight for train passengers a century ago. They fell into several groups, either with stationary or mobile residences. The most common were the

Ron V. Nixon, photographer, MOR RVN 20385

Track workers begin preparations to install new rail, on June 25, 1956, near Garrison. A large track gang is unloading welded rail that will replace the jointed rail in use. The joints between thirty-nine-foot-long rails were the most vulnerable part of track and needed frequent attention. In the mid-twentieth century, new technology for welding rails into quarter-mile lengths greatly reduced the maintenance previously required for jointed rails. When seen from trains, track crews stood in the right-of-way, enjoying a break from work.

Robert C. Morrison, photographer, MHS, PAc 95-70, B 18 F 12

"Extra gangs" worked on track projects that were too large to be done by the smaller section crews located along the line. The extra gangs moved with their work, living in work trains of "outfit" cars adapted for housing and meals as well as storage of tools and supplies. While most of the workers were single men, the families of married men also lived in the cars. These trains were parked on sidings or spur tracks close to the current project. The location shown is unknown but may be in or near Miles City, the residence of the photographer Robert C. Morrison.

section crews. Less common were the "extra gangs," with dozens of workers who took on major tasks, such as replacing many miles of rail or crossties; they lived near their projects in railcars ("outfit" or camp cars) adapted as workers' bunk and dining cars and parked on sidings. Bridge-and-building crews also lived in outfit cars, and they worked on the construction and major tasks of maintenance and alteration of, as the name conveys, bridges, buildings, and other structures, such as water tanks and coaling towers.

Stoyan Christowe described the large extra gang on the Great Northern main line in northern Montana as they stood aside and watched a train pass: "The men, holding claw bars, line bars, line wrenches, spike [mauls], adzes, tongs, and standing upon the embankment, looked like an armed savage tribe watching a vessel steaming up to the shore of their island."[25]

CHAPTER 6

Railroad Decline and the Loss to Communities

I seem to have been born with an aptitude for a way of life that was doomed, although I did not understand that at the time.

—Wendell Berry, *The Long-Legged House*

BY SEVERAL MEASURES of extent and operations, railroads in the United States reached a peak in the second half of the 1910s. The First World War brought heightened business to the rails, before competition from transport on publicly funded roads and inland waterways began to make significant inroads on rail traffic.

The long decline of railroads and other aspects of the larger world they served began in the 1910s with the convergence of several factors. Dan Cushman, born in 1909, put some of those reasons in the voice of a youth in his novel *The Grand and the Glorious* (1963). His list of factors included two that directly contributed to the railroads' decline: "Looking back, one can see that 1916 was the close of an era. Whether one attributes it to the war, the automobile, the aeroplane, the end of the Western frontier, or national Prohibition, or all of them, it can now be seen that in 1916 a whole way of life was running over the edge."[1]

The decline in railway operations and traffic was clear by the early 1920s, and by some measures—for instance, route mileage, employment, and the number of communities and businesses served by rail—it continues to the present. The reasons for nearly a century of rail decline remain contentious, with responsibility attributed to a mixture of technological change, choices of individual travelers and shippers, federal transportation policies, and conservative railroad managers and union leaders.[2] But even people with differing explanations might agree with this summary: newly developed or recently improved modes of transportation offered advantages to both travelers and shippers that railroads could not match—a combination of speed, flexibility in routes and schedules, and government-built roads, navigable waterways, and air terminals.

The internal combustion engine was the primary technological agent of change. It was, in contrast to external-combustion steam, small and durable enough to fit in sturdy, affordable personal vehicles that could travel on rough roads. Automobiles combined privacy with other factors that were also applicable to motor trucks: almost unlimited flexibility and options in routes, stops, side trips, and terminals. Governments responded to increasing levels of auto ownership by tapping public willingness to pay fuel taxes to improve road surfaces and alignments into all-weather routes. With an automobile on decent roads, a trip to and business in a town ten or twenty miles away could be done in a few hours. With more reliable vehicles and ever improving roads and highways, motor vehicles also became the preferred means for travel beyond local destinations. Motorists drove past small stores in closer (and fading) towns to reach the greater number of retail choices at larger distant places.

As one traveling salesman, in a Rock Island Railway coach, says in Meredith Willson's *The Music Man*:

> Why it's the Model T Ford made the trouble, made the people wanna go, wanna get, wanna get, wanna get up and go seven, eight, nine, ten, twelve, fourteen, twenty-two, twenty-three miles to the county seat. . . .
>
> Who's gonna patronize a little bitty two-by-four kinda store anymore?[3]

In Montana, the number of registered vehicles increased rapidly during the 1910s. General prosperity in the early part of that decade and the war-driven economy starting in 1914–15 made possible purchases by farmers and townspeople that might have been unimaginable in the first decade of the century. From 1,030 automobiles and trucks in Montana in 1910, the number grew fourteen-fold to 14,520 in 1915 and then another four-fold to 60,650 in 1920. Auto ownership in Montana grew nearly sixty-fold during the decade, while the population grew from 376,053 to 548,889, a 46 percent increase.[4]

One example of the transition from rail to road is from Montana's Hi-Line. The F. A. Buttrey department store, founded in Havre in 1902, regularly refunded the price of rail tickets to those who rode the train to shop in Havre and made purchases at the store. In the 1920s, however, Buttrey began a bus operation that paralleled the Great Northern main line in both directions. According to a local history account, Buttrey "bought a white bus and made trips to Harlem [to the east] and Gildford [to the west] to pick up those who wished to do their shopping in Havre, spending the day here and then returning the shoppers to their homes at the end of the day."[5]

The increasing use of private automobiles and commercial motor buses spurred the great dispersal of people as, in contrast to before, distances increased between places of residence, work, shopping, and entertainment, with people often living many miles, and more commuting time, away from places they visited regularly, often daily. Sprawling development along a multiplicity of roads and streets, only accessible to motor vehicles, replaced previously concentrated linear patterns of residential development along lines of steam and newer electric railways. For those familiar with compact towns and proximity of people and businesses, the physical sprawl of towns, cities, and suburbs resulted in the loosening of social life and community coherence. A specialist in local and regional history noted that this change was part of a larger trend in the diminishing of "older places (villages, valleys, regions, towns, and even city centers and neighborhoods) [that] have vanished or relinquished much of their economic, cultural, and political autonomy" to newer features such as "outpost service centers [for instance, interstate highway interchanges], immense metropolitan cities, and expanding suburbs."[6]

Another vital factor in the decline of railways was the federal government's unprecedented growing level of involvement in freight and passenger transportation, with policy preferences and funding modes favoring transport that competed with railways.

During World War I, the federal government began the engineering of some rivers, primarily the Mississippi, through dredging, the construction of locks and dams, and navigational guidance.[7] Some bulk shippers of coal, metallic ores, grain, and chemicals then shifted their cargoes from railways to barges on inland waterways. Subsidies to airlines, as vital expanding businesses, included generous payments for carrying airmail and for local government ownership and operation of airports.[8]

However, the federal government's biggest contribution to the railroad's decline was providing major funding for the construction, improvement, and maintenance of roads. It began, in 1916, with significant financial assistance to the states for road construction. Of course, public roads—unlike privately owned rail lines—were open to all individual vehicle owners and commercial operators. While drivers and operators paid fuel taxes toward the costs of construction and repair, each private and commercial user paid only a tiny portion of the total cost. One critic wrote:

> After World War II, government became the railroads' biggest competitor, as first Congress and then the White House jumped into the transportation business. . . .
>
> The public promotion of roads and [airport] runways, with government construction, government maintenance, government policing, and government signaling, made it easy for truckers and airlines and bus companies—not to speak of motorists—to compete with railroads that built and maintained their own rights of way.[9]

Well into the mid-twentieth century, railroads performed their variety of services, with the public still attracted to trains and stations. Indian River, Michigan, was a resort town located near the north end of the New York Central line between Detroit and the Straits of Mackinac. In 1949, the overnight passenger train heading south still carried perishables in express cars to wholesale and processing firms in Detroit: boxes of iced fish from commercial fishermen in nearby Petoskey and cans of cream from dairy farmers. And on summer evenings at the NYC station: "Much of the local population had come to socialize and watch the night train arrive and depart. They gathered in groups along the iron-pipe railing that edged the little park, and merged with the waiting passengers in the station and on the platform."[10]

In Montana, the last presidential candidate to visit the state by rail was Dwight Eisenhower in 1952. He rode an eighteen-car train, the "Look Ahead, Neighbor" special, across Montana, accompanied by U.S. senator Zales Ecton, who was seeking (in vain) reelection. About two thousand people in Livingston saw Eisenhower speak from the train, as did more than five thousand in Bozeman. In nearby settings, at least two groups gathered at the tracks to see the train go by: about eighty-five students from the Mount Ellis Academy east of Bozeman went to the Bear Canyon road crossing, and forty families congregated at Willow Creek, southwest of Three Forks.[11]

Composer and musician Philip Aaberg (born 1949) grew up in Chester, Montana, on the Great Northern main line west of Havre.

Ron V. Nixon, photographer, MOR RVN 11153

In the mid- to late twentieth century, the last run of a scheduled passenger train brought extra attention from railroaders, rail fans, frequent passengers, and even those who rarely rode the train but liked its regular presence. In April 1941, the Northern Pacific ended its daily-except-Sunday train over the Bitterroot Mountains between Missoula and Wallace, Idaho. Autos and buses on adjacent U.S. Route 10 had taken most of its business. On April 18, 1941, photographer Ron Nixon stayed ahead of the final westbound train No. 255 in his automobile, taking almost twenty photographs along its route. In this photo, the train pauses under the wires of the Milwaukee Road main line at Haugan, ninety-seven miles west of Missoula. (NP trains used the Milwaukee Road main line for nineteen miles east of Haugan after a flood washed out the parallel NP line.) The "1735" on the pole at the right edge of the photograph is a milepost number showing the distance from Chicago. The man on the station platform holding a bag appears to be talking with a person in the door of the Railway Post Office part of the mail-express car.

Carroll Van West, photographer, image 9052, used by permission

The train station at Chester on the former Great Northern's main line west of Havre in July 2017. Musician Philip Aaberg took the train in the 1960s to Spokane for piano lessons from this building. While the last scheduled passenger train stopped here in 1971, the BNSF Railway still uses the station for maintenance and communications purposes.

In the 1960s, GN's premier *Empire Builder* stopped in Chester on its transcontinental run. Accordingly, "when, as a young boy, he surpassed the local piano teachers, his mother, Helen Ann, put him on a train to Spokane every other Sunday through Tuesday so he could study under Julliard-trained Margaret Saunders Ott."[12] The train trip between Chester and Spokane was scheduled to take between ten hours (westbound) and ten and one-half hours (eastbound), with very late evening train times at Spokane.

The Passenger Train Problem

Historian Richard Saunders noted that in the mid-twentieth century, passenger trains were an aspect of railway services and operations that companies could not easily discard as costs rose and revenues fell. There were constraints involving both regulations and public perceptions:

> The passenger problem was not irrelevant. It cast a pall over all railroading. It was the passenger train that linked

> the railroad to the public at large, to excitement and glamour and moments of passage in people's lives. It was what set the railroads apart from other, mundane industries. As the passenger train faded, the railroad itself began to fade from the public consciousness.[13]

Projects and decisions of the federal government perhaps caused the most damage to the network of passenger trains still operating in midcentury. The biggest was the Interstate Highway System, created by an act of Congress in 1956 and largely constructed across Montana during the 1960s. Interstate highways made possible hours of uninterrupted fast travel for trucks and motorists, bypassing towns and cities that had previously slowed highway travel. The 360 miles of U.S. Route 10 between Billings and Missoula illustrate the incremental change as portions of Interstate 90 were completed and eventually connected. Before the interstate, motorists had to slow or stop in twenty-one places: cities such as Butte and Bozeman, towns like Belgrade and Deer Lodge, and smaller communities, Reed Point and Logan. In a novel by Ivan Doig, a character remarks about a road trip in 1954, "Interstate freeways hadn't yet bisected the West, and the highway went through towns, so that you felt you were visiting each one."[14]

The construction of the interstate highways in Montana began slowly. In 1961, five years after congressional approval, there had been very little work done replacing U.S. 10 in southern Montana—only a short section of divided highway that bypassed Butte and Rocker, just to the west. After ten years of intensive construction, in 1971, completed sections of I-90 went around fifteen places between Billings and Missoula. Remaining portions of U.S. 10 still carried through traffic on the main streets of just six communities.[15]

The interstate that bypassed these towns also took traffic from the Northern Pacific trains that stopped in those same towns. A retired official with the Northern Pacific recalled the impact on NP passenger trains in Montana, in contrast to the Great Northern: "The NP was eventually paralleled by Interstate highways 90 and 94, whereas the Great Northern had US Highway 2 paralleling it. The Interstate system had a substantial adverse impact on the NP's short haul traffic, such as Billings to Butte. The Great Northern was less impacted than the NP."[16] The loss of sustaining traffic was particularly apparent on NP secondary transcontinental trains Nos. 1

and 2, the *Mainstreeter,* which carried lots of mail and express and travelers, most making trips of short and middle distances. "Coach business could be brisk during summer, college break times and periods of inclement weather. But as Interstate 90 crept across the Northern states, and Northwest Orient [Airlines] learned how to keep the wings from falling off its Lockheed Electras, passenger loadings on Nos. 1 and 2 dropped."[17]

A different, and crucial, government action was the removal of the U.S. mail from railways. From the mid-1800s, trains had provided the primary inland means of moving mail. By the mid-twentieth century, as fewer people rode passenger trains, the carriage of mail and express in head-end cars provided increasingly vital revenue. By 1967, mail traffic provided the Great Northern—especially mail on the combined *Western Star–Fast Mail* secondary transcontinental run—with 44 percent of its passenger train revenues.[18] As late as the summer of 1966, GN's westbound *Western Star–Fast Mail* regularly left St. Paul with twenty-three cars: the nine cars for passengers (coaches, sleepers, and food and beverage service) outnumbered by the thirteen cars of mail and express, with one coach at the end of the train for the crew.[19]

By the late 1950s, however, early losses of mail and express traffic to trucks and airplanes contributed to the end of some passenger trains in Montana, such as the Milwaukee Road's *Olympian Hiawatha,* and trains on Great Northern secondary lines centered on Great Falls. The biggest shock occurred in 1967 when the U.S. Post Office announced its decision to replace the sorting of mail by clerks while in transit with processing in regional centers equipped with automated optical devices. This change ended the function of railway post offices as well as the carriage of nearly all remaining mail by passenger trains. First-class mail increasingly shifted to air transport, and lower priority mail shifted to fast freight trains and trucks. Railroads across the United States responded by quickly seeking to end operations of many passenger trains. *Trains* magazine editor David P. Morgan, combining consideration of ocean liners and passenger trains, remarked of 1967, "Last year a travel era, a way of mobile life, a system of going places, if you will, began to disintegrate as, one by one, the *Queen Mary* departed Pier 90, New York, for the last time," and a long list of railroads announced they would seek government approval for drastic cutbacks, or even total elimination, of their passenger trains.[20] By 1970, the dismal future of passenger trains led the federal government to create the National Rail Passenger Corporation, better known as Amtrak. In May 1971, it took over operation of many of the trains then still running.

While much of the decline of railroads in passenger and freight service was due to loss of business, changes within railroading also diminished the presence of railways on the landscape and in society. Railroads strongly advanced mechanization and automation in operations, maintenance, communications, and traffic control, centralizing these functions in a small number of towns and cities. Many "railroad towns" lost their rail employment and the features that had been part of their identity for decades. In contrast to steam, diesel-electric locomotives required far fewer people and facilities in operations and maintenance. Freight train crews shrank from five to just two people, and they worked longer distances, passing through former crew-change towns. Examples in Montana include Cut Bank on the former Great Northern (now BNSF) and Livingston on the former Northern Pacific (now Missoula-based Montana Rail Link). With smaller crews and partial automation, a part of railroads that the public favored—the conductor and brakeman waving from

Photographer unknown, MHS, PAc 86-15.63166L

An aerial view, looking west, of Reed Point, midway between Billings and Livingston, in August 1963. At the center of the photograph are the Northern Pacific main line and the two-lane U.S. Route 10. Both appear small in contrast to the construction excavation and earthwork that nearly fills the three-hundred-foot-wide right-of-way for Interstate 90 curving around the south edge of town. In this part of the Yellowstone Valley, many landowners opposed the freeway project because of the large scale of land acquisition for the right-of-way.

A Northern Pacific caboose at Billings in about 1908. A familiar sight into the 1980s was the caboose at the end of all freight trains. In this car, the conductor and rear brakeman, also called the flagman, spent much of their time in the cupola watching the train ahead for problems. On freight trains in local service, they did switching at spur and industry tracks. The caboose included a work desk for the conductor, a stove for heat and cooking, and bunks for sleeping. At the time of this photo, the crew lived in the car during layovers at the terminal away from their home. Cabooses were assigned to specific conductors, some of whom decorated them, as seen by the antlers on the roof of the cupola. In the late 1980s, railways cut crew size and, with new technology, eliminated the need to have any crew at the back end of freight trains.

Photographer unknown, MOR RVN 01546

the caboose at the end of a freight train—disappeared. Large, complicated machines took over much of the track work done by section crews. Telegraphers in train order stations were replaced by radios in locomotives and remotely controlled signal systems that conveyed operating orders. Whole groups of workers lost jobs as railroads exited labor-intensive segments of the business—passengers, express, mail, and less-than-carload freight. Railroads abandoned and dismantled signature properties, including stations, roundhouses, water tanks, and track itself. Many branch lines disappeared through the middle of the twentieth century, as did, by the early 1980s, even some main lines of bankrupt companies. A notable example of the latter in Montana was the western extension and branches of the Milwaukee Road west of the Dakotas. The last trains ran on the line in March 1980, and, with a few exceptions, the tracks were removed in the next few years.

All these changes reduced or fully eliminated the presence of railroads in thousands of towns and cities in North America.[21] Even on main lines that remain busy, the railway presence has diminished greatly, and many places have neither rail employees nor businesses

shipping freight by rail. With these losses, the integral daily presence and utility of railroads and their employees have diminished in public knowledge and awareness. Perhaps all that remains in the public consciousness is annoyance with trains that sound horns at night and sometimes block street crossings.

The shrinking presence of the railways in American travel and life is evident in three stories of those particularly affected. In 1959, David Plowden sought to study under influential photographer

Ron V. Nixon, photographer, MOR RVN 20085

In the mid- to late 1950s, as railroads completed the conversion to diesel-electric power from steam, they donated a few steam locomotives to towns for public display, mostly at division points where the work of railroads had dominated the towns' economy and landscape. In Montana, Billings, Helena, Missoula, and Havre received steam engines for display in the 1950s. On a rainy November 10, 1955, the president of the Northern Pacific formally presented Missoula with steam locomotive No. 1356. This engine, built in 1902, spent much of its working life based in that city, pulling passenger, freight, and work trains. Ron Nixon took this photograph from an upper floor of the NP passenger station and division headquarters.

Minor White. As part of his application, Plowden sent photos he had taken of his favorite subject, the remaining operating steam locomotives, which were nearing complete replacement in the United States and Canada by diesel-electric power. Decades later, he paraphrased White telling him "that all my photographs reflected a feeling of loss. The loss of the steam engine, he surmised. He was right."[22]

A caption in a 1968 book on the Union Pacific Railroad in Oregon, Washington, and northern Idaho combined the loving detail, in railroad brevity, of locomotives and trains with a final burst of bitterness:

> The chaste lines of a Harriman Pacific [steam locomotive] enhance this photographic souvenir of a Golden Age which was recorded for posterity on September 25, 1947 as the [locomotive numbered] 3206 arrived at Lewiston, Idaho on [passenger] Train 74. Such scenes were once commonplace, before the incursions of an age of psychopathic confusion, completely devoid of esthetics, destroyed the beauty that once was.[23]

Mary Clearman Blew conveyed the decline of both railroads and the human landscapes they created on Montana's northern plains, describing "one of those little towns along the Montana highline that has a couple of grain elevators and a store and a bowling alley, a town that used to have a railroad depot and still has its name in black letters on a white board that faces the rail bed where tall grass blows endlessly and the gravel streets get narrower every year."[24]

Montana: Examples from Decades of Decline

In Montana, these decades of railroad diminution were evident in many ways. The losses first appeared on a local scale. The first street railways to end operations were in Billings in 1917, followed by Bozeman in 1921, and Helena in 1927. In Anaconda, the streetcars outlasted all others in Montana, enduring until 1951. The state's sole interurban electric line, between Bozeman, Bozeman Hot Springs, and Gallatin Gateway, ended operations in 1931.[25]

Local passenger services on intercity railroads also faded quickly. One example is the rapid decline of rail service between Butte and Anaconda, twenty-six miles apart by rail. Through the 1910s and into the early 1920s, the Butte, Anaconda & Pacific ran four passenger trains each way daily between the towns. But competition from buses between Butte and Anaconda, on the first paved road in Montana, forced the BA&P to cut frequency of trains in half in 1923. By 1929, the BA&P's two daily round-trips competed with nine daily round-trips offered by the Intermountain Bus Company.[26] While passengers could ride on the BA&P into the mid-1950s, it was on a slow schedule in a passenger car at the end of a freight train that usually carried the crew and the rare passenger.[27] Railroad historian Thomas T. Taber observed and rode the mixed train in its last years of operation and described the westbound schedule out of Butte:

> Engines and [passenger] car quietly backed out of the [Milwaukee Road] station to West Butte yard where a string of loaded cars were. The train then "highballed" west another three miles to Rocker where another set of cars were cut in. The "passenger" train was then composed of upwards of seventy loads of copper ore and the coach. This switching and tonnage hardly allowed the train to make its 90 minute running time to Anaconda, but that made no difference because no one was riding it anyway. . . .
>
> The mixed train continued until April 16, 1955 when it was discontinued. Except for a few rail fans no one mourned its passing, the need for a train having vanished almost thirty years earlier.[28]

Two railroads operated daily transcontinental passenger trains through Montana until 1970. The Great Northern and Northern Pacific each ran two pairs of trains. The pattern continued under Burlington Northern, the company into which they merged, until May 1971. At that time, federally operated Amtrak took over almost all passenger trains in the United States, including between Chicago, St. Paul, and Seattle. Through most of the 1970s, Amtrak operated two trains across Montana on the Chicago-Seattle route. The *Empire Builder* was Amtrak's primary train in the northern corridor, on the former GN (now BNSF) route across northern Montana. Pressured by Montana's U.S. senator (and Senate majority leader) Mike Mansfield, Amtrak reluctantly added a second Chicago-Seattle train, the *North Coast Hiawatha,* on the former NP line (now BNSF, and west of Billings, Montana Rail Link) through the more populated southern part of the state.

During the second half of President Jimmy Carter's administration, financial constraints forced Amtrak to reduce its national network. In early October 1979, Amtrak ended operation of one Chicago-Seattle train, the *North Coast Hiawatha.* Counterintuitively, Amtrak chose to retain the *Empire Builder,* which served just one of the ten largest cities in Montana, Havre, the seventh largest.

A Crow man rides in a coach on a Burlington Route train that crossed the Crow Indian Reservation. Burlington trains linked four major communities on the reservation—Hardin, Crow Agency, Lodge Grass, and Wyola—to the nearest cities, Billings, Montana, and Sheridan, Wyoming, and points beyond. This portrait is a product of an unusual photographic project commissioned in 1948 by the Burlington Route to document the life and work of the regions it served. When the Burlington applied to federal regulators to end all passenger service on its line from Nebraska to Billings in 1969, the government of the Crow Nation formally protested, in vain, the end of passenger trains, citing the railroad's commitment to perpetual passenger transportation in the negotiations for the 1890s agreement granting the Burlington a right-of-way across the reservation.

Amtrak's Chicago-Seattle *Empire Builder* was the successor to the Great Northern train of the same name. In this June 7, 1978, photograph, the westbound train has just crossed the Continental Divide at Marias Pass on the Burlington Northern main line. By 2018, the *Empire Builder* had operated longer as an Amtrak train (forty-seven years) than as a Great Northern train (forty-one years).

Ron Nixon, photographer, MOR RVN 32739

Amtrak stated that communities on this route had few other public transport options. The end of the *North Coast Hiawatha* resulted in the withdrawal of rail passenger service to five of the ten largest (including the first, third, and fourth largest) cities in the state: Miles City, Billings, Bozeman, Butte, and Missoula. The company's official explanation was that people on this route had access to intercity buses and airlines.[29] Mike Mansfield, who had strongly promoted and protected the *North Coast Hiawatha,* had retired from the Senate in 1977 and become U.S. ambassador to Japan.

Zurich, Again, and the BNSF Railway

One of the places that sees the passage of more trains than a century ago is Zurich. Little remains of the town where young Dan

Cushman listened to train crews in his father's pool hall and watched troop trains pass. Zurich is now a tiny rural settlement with an elementary school but neither retail businesses nor railroaders. The former Great Northern main line is now the northern transcontinental main line of BNSF Railway, the product of several mergers that first absorbed the GN, Northern Pacific, and Burlington in 1970 and the Santa Fe in 1995. What remains of the railway property is just the main track, passing siding, and inactive industry spur. The station building survives, removed from the right-of-way and located on a nearby hilltop. Two dilapidated grain elevators remain along the industry track, examples of the small wood-crib "country elevators" made redundant by a small number of very large concrete or steel elevators with enough capacity to load a whole train with grain. The nearest of these to Zurich are at Harlem and Havre. William Wyckoff describes Zurich now at train time: "The train still passes, but no longer stops. . . . There is the deafening rumble of

William Wyckoff, photographer, with permission of the photographer

Zurich, Montana, with a BNSF train, in a photograph taken in July 2001. Historical geographer Bill Wyckoff replicated the location and angle of the 1922 State Highway Department photograph in chapter 3 (see page 78). The railway presence has been greatly reduced from 1922, with the depot, section base, and associated employees long gone. What remains of the busy railway are the tracks—main line, siding, industry track (with two grain elevators), the pole line, and many times a day, the trains. U.S. Route 2 had been relocated decades earlier from the historic alignment in this photograph to south of the tracks, beyond the right edge of the photo.

a train that departs as quickly as it arrives, its breathless speed a reminder of the town's modern irrelevance in the grander scheme of things."[30] Amtrak passengers might easily miss Zurich as they pass at seventy-nine miles per hour.

Degrees of Loss: Public Utility, Social Service, and Personal Nostalgia

Advocates and admirers of railways acknowledge levels of difference in their laments of loss. They realize that some losses were inevitable in the context of changing technology and business practices. Steam locomotives, narrow gauge trains, and staffed small-town stations cannot be recovered and remain only where saved by historic preservation and tourist railways. But some of the losses were neither inevitable nor inconsequential. Many abandoned rail properties and operations were neither obsolete nor without potential for revival as proponents of roads and "rails to trails" often claimed. There has been a loss of real and useful public and commercial services. Main line passenger trains are a good example. Freight trains on main and branch lines that served businesses—grain elevators, feed mills, sawmills, and lumber yards—are another. Continued rail freight service could have reduced the use of heavy trucks that cause damage to city streets and rural roads far out of proportion to their weight relative to automobiles.

There was also loss beyond the trains on the tracks providing services. Railways, and especially stations and passenger trains, became favored lenses through which to recall and lament perceived losses in the larger world of community and commerce that railroads did so much at first to create and then to sustain. Railroads represent a world many remembered as simpler, slower, more stable, and with stronger social ties and more economic services within communities. Overnight trains provided more than just transportation, but also lodging in sleeping cars and meal service while in motion. Trains and buses stopped in the center of towns close to hotels, motels, and restaurants.

The motor vehicles running on publicly funded roads are usually credited with dramatically and effectively increasing people's mobility and associated opportunities. An unspoken assumption common to planners was that outside major cities—where public funding sustained bus and rail transit systems—people would be

Sam Richards, photographer, Gallatin History Museum, Bozeman, 90.1701

The Northern Pacific operated a fifteen-mile-long branch line in the Gallatin Valley—from Manhattan on the NP main line to Anceny—that primarily served farming and ranching. By the mid-1980s, freight traffic had nearly disappeared, and the Burlington Northern received permission to abandon the line. On October 19, 1985, Sam Richards, a reporter for the Belgrade weekly newspaper, took this photograph of the second-to-last train on the branch at Amsterdam, a single diesel and four loaded grain hopper cars. The track was dismantled the following spring.

willing to use their cars in all circumstances. Furthermore, there was apparently a belief that cars, trucks, and buses could efficiently handle all the traffic anticipated by even the most optimistic proponents of growth. However, for those unable or unwilling to use automobiles all the time and in all weather, declines in rail service meant there was a loss of mobility. Privately operated, scheduled ground transport diminished in routes and frequency and in many cases disappeared, especially far from cities. Governments at all levels made few provisions to support or sustain public ground transportation. Or, as one harsh critic of "the highwaymen" (his term for "the highway-motor complex") stated, "The new highwaymen robbed the world's most affluent nation of a choice how to get from here to there." Furthermore, policy presumed "that people would opt for motor over rail travel for *all* their needs—commuting, shopping, business travel, recreation."[31]

The loss extended to all public transport. In 2018, two towns in Montana, each with a population of over five thousand people, have no scheduled public transportation—rail, bus, or air: Anaconda with about nine thousand residents and Lewistown with about six thousand. Lewistown is also the largest town in Montana (ranked fifteenth by population) without any rail connection or service. BNSF dismantled the tracks into Lewistown in 2006, just over a century after the first rail line reached the town.[32]

Public attitudes in recent decades have, in some cases, moved from seeing railways as an accepted part of a community to general indifference and even opposition to railways and train traffic. It is part of the larger attitude of NIMBY ("not in my back yard"), an antipathy toward activities and entities that are considered dirty, noisy, smelly, or otherwise intrusive in residential and retail districts:

> While railroads have less [harmful environmental] impact than trucks overall, their impacts are more concentrated. Freight trains make noise, spew fumes, create vibrations, and sometimes carry hazardous or smelly cargo. They blast their horns at grade crossings, back up traffic, and delay fire engines and emergency vehicles. . . . Homeowners worry that freight trains hurt their property values.[33]

In Montana, for example, opposition has grown to trains carrying certain cargoes—in particular, to proposed increased frequency of solid trains of coal and crude oil on the former Northern Pacific main line. The Northern Plains Resource Council, based in Billings, published the booklet *The True Costs of Coal Exports,* targeting the proposed increase of railway coal traffic from the Powder River Basin in eastern Montana and Wyoming as well as to the destination export terminals in western Washington. It mentioned potential damage to health from both locomotive exhaust and coal dust blowing off loads in open hopper cars: "If the proposed export terminals were permitted and built, every community along the 1,500-mile transport route would experience the damaging health impacts of elevated levels of both coal dust and diesel particulates."[34] The issue remains unresolved.

CONCLUSION

Railway Survivors

NO ONE has been able to ride a scheduled train to Danvers, as Mary Clearman Blew's aunt did during the Second World War, since 1955. However, one can still ride a train *through* the site of Danvers without stopping. After the Milwaukee Road went bankrupt and withdrew from central Montana in 1980, the track northwest of Lewistown became the state-supported Central Montana Rail, intended primarily to haul grain. Since the first years of the 2000s, passengers can ride a summer season dinner train, the Charlie Russell Chew-Choo, from a junction north of Lewistown through Danvers to Denton and return. There is little evidence at Danvers of the former town, but an alert passenger might notice the two country grain elevators. The Chew-Choo is regularly stopped and "robbed" by riders on horses. In her novel *Jackalope Dreams,* Blew incorporated a fictional version of the dinner train and the locals on horseback who played train robbers.[1]

The last trains on the Milwaukee Road main line through Harlowton departed in March 1980, slowly heading eastward on track that would be dismantled within a few years. The railroad legacy of Harlowton survives in several ways. One is the mascot name of Harlowton High School teams, the Engineers. It was adopted when Harlowton was a booming railroad division point at the east end of the Rocky Mountain section of electrified transcontinental main line, and the name now recalls that past. Another is at the intersection of Central Avenue with U.S. Highway 12, where there is a small park with a boxy electric locomotive, numbered E57B, that shunted cars in the switchyard on the south edge of town until 1974. The E57B provided the Engineers with a backdrop in 2001 when, that fall, the Harlowton High School girls basketball team took second place at the state Class C tournament. A few days later, the *Harlowton Times-Clarion* had on its front page a photo with the caption, "The Lady Engineers rode a float in the Christmas Lights Parade Sunday evening and stopped long enough to pose for a photograph at the E-57B engine in Fischer Park."[2]

Notes

Photograph Credit Abbreviations

MHS: Photograph Archives, Montana Historical Society Research Center, Helena
MOR: Museum of the Rockies, Bozeman, Montana
MSU: Archives and Special Collections, Renne Library, Montana State University, Bozeman
RVN: Ron V. Nixon Collection, MOR
UM: Archives and Special Collections, Mansfield Library, University of Montana, Missoula

Epigraph

Trains, June 1982, 22.

Introduction

1. Ivan Doig, "You Can't Not Go Home Again," *Montana The Magazine of Western History* 35:1 (1985): 6 n.5. The Ringling station survived until 2016, when it was demolished to salvage the wood.
2. *Statement Regarding Proposed Discontinuance of Milwaukee Road Trains No. 15 and No. 16, the Olympian Hiawatha, between Minneapolis and Seattle-Tacoma* (Chicago: The Milwaukee Road, 1960), 7.
3. Doig, "You Can't Not Go," 6.
4. Ivan Doig, *This House of Sky: Landscapes of a Western Mind* (San Diego: Harcourt Brace Jovanovich, 1978), 244.
5. Tom Murray, *The Milwaukee Road* (St. Paul: MBI, 2005), 122, 131–34, 145.
6. Joseph P. Schwieterman, *When the Railroad Leaves Town: American Communities in the Age of Rail Line Abandonment, Western United States* (Kirksville, MO: Truman State University Press, 2004), xv.
7. John H. White Jr., *The American Railroad Passenger Car,* pt. 1 (Baltimore: The Johns Hopkins University Press, 1978), xi.
8. Hal Borland, *Country Editor's Boy* (Philadelphia: J. B. Lippincott Company, 1970), 23.
9. Ibid., 157.

10. Mary Clearman Blew, *Writing Her Own Life: Imogene Welch, Western Rural Schoolteacher* (Norman: University of Oklahoma Press, 2004), 127.
11. *Bozeman (MT) Chronicle*, Aug. 15, 2003, A4.

Chapter 1

1. Dale Martin, "Still the 'Main Street of the Northwest': The Continuing Legacy of the Northern Pacific Railway in Montana" (paper presented at Creating Space: Across Histories, Cultures, and Disciplines conference, Big Sky, MT, Sept. 23–26, 2004; *Bozeman (MT) Chronicle*, Sept. 26, 2004, A1.
2. Bryan Morgan, *Civil Engineering: Railways* (London: Longman, 1971), 37; Andrew C. O'Dell and Peter S. Richards, *Railways and Geography*, 2d ed. (London: Hutchinson University Library, 1971), 17–20, 78–94.
3. *First Annual Report of the Board of Railroad Commissioners of the State of Montana Covering the Period between March 1, 1907 and August 31, 1908* (Helena, MT: State Publishing Company, [1908]), 235–48.
4. *General Laws and Constitutional Provisions of the State of Montana Relating to Railroad, Express, Sleeping Car . . . Companies . . .* (Helena, MT: Railroad and Public Service Commission of Montana, 1913), 42.
5. Morgan, *Civil Engineering*, 37; Ross Ralph Cotroneo, "The History of the Northern Pacific Land Grant, 1900–1952" (PhD diss., University of Idaho, 1966), 147.
6. Alfred D. Chandler Jr., ed. and comp., *The Railroads: The Nation's First Big Business, Sources and Readings* (New York: Harcourt, Brace & World, Inc., 1965), 9.
7. Mallory Hope Ferrell, "Utah & Northern, the Narrow Gauge That Opened a Frontier," in *Colorado Rail Annual No. 15: Idaho Montana Issue* (Golden, CO: Colorado Railroad Museum, 1981), 15, 26, 56.
8. *Appletons' Annual Cyclopaedia and Register of Important Events of the Year 1883*, n.s., vol. 8 (New York: D. Appleton and Company, 1884), 761–63; *Travelers' Official Guide of the Railways*, July 1883, 255, 263.
9. John R. Stilgoe, *Metropolitan Corridor: Railroads and the American Scene* (New Haven, CT: Yale University Press, 1983), 203, 205.
10. Northern Pacific Railway, *2000 Miles of Scenic Beauty* (St. Paul, MN, Great Northern Railway, 1929), 34.
11. Federal Writers' Project, *Montana: A State Guide Book*, rev. ed. (New York, Hasting's House, 1949), 246, 334. On the Milwaukee Road, the boundary between Pacific and Mountain time zones was at Avery, Idaho.
12. Slason Thompson, preparer, *Railway Statistics of the United States of America for the Year Ended December 31, 1926* (Chicago: Bureau of Railway News and Statistics, 1927), 60; U.S. Bureau of the Census, *Fourteenth Census of the United States Taken in the Year 1920, Vol. 4. Population 1920: Occupations* (Washington, DC: GPO, 1923), 34–43.
13. *First Biennial Report of the Department of Labor and Industry, 1913–1914* (Helena, MT: Independent Publishing Co., n.d.), 183–91, 195–203.
14. O'Dell and Richards, *Railways and Geography*, 226–29. On western railroad-shaped landscapes, see Robert G. Athearn, *Union Pacific Country* (Chicago: Rand McNally & Company, 1971).
15. James R. Shortridge, *Our Town on the Plains: J. J. Pennell's Photographs of Junction City, Kansas, 1893–1922* (Lawrence: University Press of Kansas, 2000), 22, 195.
16. John C. Hudson, *Plains Country Towns* (Minneapolis: University of Minnesota

Press, 1985), 58; Theodore Macklin, *Efficient Marketing for Agriculture: Its Services, Methods, and Agencies* (New York: Macmillan Company, 1921), 120 (table 16).

17. *Twelfth Annual Report of the Board of Railroad Commissioners . . . of the State of Montana [for] Year Ended November 30, 1919* (Helena, MT: Independent Publishing Co., n.d.), 59–61. For a list of the major commodities, with dollar value of Montana output, in the mid-1910s, see *Montana 1915* (Helena, MT: Montana Department of Agriculture and Publicity, [1915]), 92. The top five commodities by value were copper, wheat, hay, beef cattle, and zinc.
18. Thomas Curtis Clarke et al., *The American Railway: Its Construction, Development, Management, and Appliances* (New York: C. Scribner's Sons, 1888, 1897; reprint, New York: Arno Press, 1976), 432. A map of the national rail network in 1880, from *Scribner's Statistical Atlas* (New York: Charles Scribner's Sons, 1880), shows Montana with the least (and last reached) mileage of all states and territories. The second-to-last territory or state to be reached by rail was New Mexico, in 1879.
19. *Reports of Cases and Proceedings before the Board of Railroad Commissioners of the State of Montana*, vol. 13 (Helena, MT: Independent Publishing Co., 1920), 137. An overview account of the development of the network of main lines in Montana is included in Michael P. Malone, Richard B. Roeder, and William L. Lang, *Montana: A History of Two Centuries*, rev. ed. (Seattle: University of Washington Press, 1993), 172–84, 282 (map).
20. The term "High Line" appeared in print as early as 1916 in the state promotional publication *The Resources and Opportunities of Montana* (Helena, MT: Independent Publishing Co., 1916), 18 (photo caption).
21. O'Dell and Richards, *Railways and Geography*, 146–50.
22. The density of transcontinental railroads in Montana is especially apparent in the map in James E. Vance Jr., *Capturing the Horizon: The Historical Geography of Transportation since the Transportation Revolution of the Sixteenth Century* (New York: Harper & Row, 1986), 317.
23. Robert G. Athearn, "A View from the High Country," *Western Historical Quarterly* 2:2 (1971): 127–28.
24. An early overview of Montana's short lines, including accounts of the author's visits to some of the lines, is found in Thomas T. Taber, "Short Lines of the Treasure State: The Histories of the Independently Operated Railroads of Montana," April 1960, TS, Montana Historical Society, Helena.
25. U.S. Bureau of the Census, *Fourteenth Census of the United States Taken in the Year 1920, Vol. 1. Population: 1920* (Washington, DC: GPO, 1921), 249–50, 499–508.
26. Murray, *The Milwaukee Road*, 42–44, 53 (photo of Chicago, Milwaukee & St. Paul Railway public timetable cover, Dec. 1922–Jan. 1923).
27. Electric, intercity, and street electric railways are surveyed in "Montana's Trolleys," published in Ira L. Swett's *Interurbans Magazine* 26:3 (1969); 26:4 (1969); 27:1 (1970).
28. U.S. Department of the Interior, National Park Service, *General Information Regarding Yellowstone National Park 1919 Season June 20 to September 15* (Washington, DC: GPO, 1919), 17–19.
29. C. W. Guthrie, *All Aboard! for Glacier: The Great Northern Railway and Glacier National Park* (Helena, MT: Farcountry Press, 2004), 59–77.
30. Great Northern Railway, *Time Tables* (St. Paul, MN: Great Northern Railway, 1920), corrected to July 11, 1920, 19; U.S. Bureau of the Census, *Fourteenth Census, Vol. 1*, 499–500, 503, 505, 506, 508.
31. Information derived from "List of Airports in Montana," www.wikipedia.com; www.

amtrak.com; saltlakeexpress.com; www.jeffersonlines.com; locations.greyhound.com.

Chapter 2

1. William Allen White, *The Autobiography of William Allen White* (New York: Macmillan Company, 1946), 257.
2. Ida (Simpson) Waylett, "Trains and Semans," in *Always a Hometown: Semans and District History* (Semans, SK: Semans and District Historical Society, 1982), 8.
3. Alice Munro, "Working for a Living," in *The View from Castle Rock* (New York: Alfred A. Knopf, 2006), 169.
4. Lyle Johnston, *"Good Night, Chet": A Biography of Chet Huntley* (Jefferson, NC: McFarland & Company, Inc., 2003), 8–9; Chet Huntley, *The Generous Years: Remembrances of a Frontier Boyhood* (New York: Random House, 1968), 135, 147–55, 160.
5. Huntley, *Generous Years*, 193.
6. *The Consolidated Code of Operating Rules and General Instructions*, 1945 ed. (issued jointly by several railroads of the north-central and northwestern United States, including the Milwaukee, Great Northern, and Northern Pacific), 7.
7. "Autobiography of Emmett B. Moore," 46, 48, 1973, TS, copy in author's possession; Emmett Moore Jr., letter to the author, May 12, 2017.
8. "Railway Stations and Architecture," *Railway Review*, Nov. 27, 1915, 692.
9. For sources of station names on the Milwaukee Road's lines, see August Derleth, *The Milwaukee Road: Its First Hundred Years* (New York: Creative Age Press, 1948), 182–84.
10. Roberta Carkeek Cheney, *Names on the Face of Montana: The Story of Montana's Place Names* (Missoula, MT: Mountain Press Publishing Company, 1984), 129; Rich Aarstad, Ellie Arguimbau, Ellen Baumler, Charlene Porsild, and Brian Shovers, *Montana Place Names from Alzada to Zortman* (Helena, MT: Montana Historical Society Press, 2009), 71.
11. *Reports of Cases . . .* 1920, 59.
12. Herbert L. Pease, *Singing Rails* (New York: Thomas Y. Crowell, 1948), 27.
13. *Official Guide of the Railways*, June 1916, 629.
14. Northern Pacific Railway, "N.P. R'y. Standard Plan of Telegraph Office with Living Rooms," Plan M.44-10 (ca. 1905), copy in author's collection.
15. *U.S. Statutes at Large*, vol. 34, pt. 1 (1907), 1415–17 (Hours of Service Law).
16. Eugene Manlove Rhodes, *Stepsons of Light* (Boston: Houghton Mifflin Company, 1921), 128.
17. Grant Burns, *The Railroad in American Fiction: An Annotated Bibliography* (Jefferson, NC: McFarland & Company, Inc., 2005), 12, 34–43; John R. Stilgoe, "Sounders and Silence: Some Isolated Train-Order Stations in Fiction," *Railroad History* 157 (Autumn 1987): 48–49.
18. The following material is from Cornelius W. Hauck, "Union Pacific Montana Division," *Colorado Rail Annual* 15, 104–5; Thornton Waite, *Union Pacific: Montana Division, Route of the Butte Special* (Columbia, MO, and Idaho Falls, ID: Brueggenjohann/reese, Inc. & Thornton Waite, 1998), 142–69.
19. Burton K. Wheeler, with Paul F. Healy, *Yankee from the West* (Garden City, NY: Doubleday & Company, Inc., 1962), 173–75.
20. Bradley Snow, interview with author, Bozeman, MT, Oct. 13, 2016.
21. White, *American Railroad Passenger Car*, pt. 1, xii.

22. On railroads, the art they commissioned, and publicity for national parks, see Kirby Lambert, "The Lure of the Parks," *Montana The Magazine of Western History* 46:1 (1996): cover, 1, 42–55, quote on 46.
23. Carlos A. Schwantes, *Railroad Signatures across the Pacific Northwest* (Seattle: University of Washington Press, 1993), 109–20, 193–204.
24. Don Baker, *The Montana Railroad Alias: The Jawbone* (Boulder, CO: Fred Pruett, 1990), 87.
25. White, *American Railroad Passenger Car*, pt. 1, xi.
26. *Tenth Annual Report of the Board of Railroad Commissioners and Ex-Officio Public Service Commission of the State of Montana [for] Year Ending November 30, 1917* (Helena, MT: Independent Publishing Co., n.d.), 140–50, quotes on 140–41, 146, 147.
27. George H. Drury, comp., *The Historical Guide to North American Railroads* (Milwaukee: Kalmbach Publishing Co., 1985), 272–73.
28. Meredith Willson, "Wells Fargo Wagon," song from *The Music Man* (New York: Hal Leonard, 1962).
29. Mark T. Smokov, *He Rode with Butch and Sundance: The Story of Harvey "Kid Curry" Logan* (Denton: University of North Texas Press, 2012), 185–200.
30. The story is included in the collection by Dorothy M. Johnson, *The Hanging Tree and Other Stories* (New York: Ballantine Books, 1957), 143–55.
31. Brian W. Dippie, ed., *Charles M. Russell, Word Painter: Letters 1887–1926* (Fort Worth, TX: Amon Carter Museum, 1993), 36, 45.
32. Waylett, "Trains," 8.
33. The process is illustrated in a sequence of photos taken in southern California, in Richard Steinheimer, "Mrs. Adkins Meets No. 51," *Classic Trains*, Fall 2006, 42–47.
34. William B. Cook, "Mileposts: Topographic Mapping with the U.S. Geological Survey 1954–77," 22, TS memoir in possession of author.
35. Stoyan Christowe, *My American Pilgrimage* (Boston: Little, Brown and Company, 1947), 196–97.
36. Ibid., 200.
37. Richard Reinhardt, ed., *Workin' on the Railroad: Reminiscences from the Age of Steam* (Palo Alto, CA: American West Publishing Company, 1970), 209.
38. *First Biennial Report of the Department of Labor and Industry, 1913–1914*, 195–203.
39. E. E. Russell Tratman, *Railway Track and Track Work* (New York: McGraw-Hill Book Company, 1909), 284–85, 291–93, 296–97.
40. Borland, *Country Editor's Boy*, 259–60.
41. Thomas Bell, *Out of This Furnace* (New York: Little, Brown and Company, 1941; reprint, Pittsburgh: University of Pittsburgh Press, 1976), 20–21.
42. Northern Pacific Railway, "N.P. Ry. Standard Plan of Bunk House for 16 Men with Living Room," Plan S-39-80 (1905), in "Note" below title block, copy in author's collection.
43. Harry Bedwell, "Back in Circulation," *Railroad Magazine*, Aug. 1940, 92.

Chapter 3

1. *Bozeman (MT) Chronicle*, June 7, 2015, C2.
2. *First Annual Report of the Board of Railroad Commissioners of the State of Montana, 1907–1908*, 298.
3. "Railway Stations and Architecture," *Railway Review*, Nov. 27, 1915, 692.

4. H. Roger Grant, "The Country Railroad Station in the West," *Journal of the West* 17:4 (1978): 32.
5. Ibid.
6. Ibid., 33–36.
7. "C.M.&St.P. Ry., Bridge & Building Dep't, [standard plan of] "24'-0" x 60'-0" Depot" (Jan. 1902), reproduced in Grant, "Country Railroad Station," 33.
8. "N.P.R.R. Standard Plan of Class-C-2 Story Combination Depot" (1890, rev. 1891), Plan S-26-29, reproduced in Chuck Soule, "Standard Plan Two-Story Depots, Part 1: 1889–1890, French Hip Style," *The Mainstreeter* 25:4 (2006): 10, 11.
9. *On the Track of History: Brady, Montana in the 20th Century 1909–1999* (Brady, MT: Brady History Book Committee, 1999), 42.
10. "Dean of the Railroaders," in *1913–1948 Anniversary Album of the Scobey Community, Daniels County, Montana* (Scobey, MT: Junior Chamber of Commerce of Scobey, MT, 1948), n.p.
11. *Reports of Cases . . . 1920*, 83.
12. Dan Cushman, *Plenty of Room & Air* (Great Falls, MT: Stay Away, Joe Publishers, 1975), 188, 190.
13. Ibid., 192–93.
14. Great Northern Railway, station plat "Glasgow-Pacific Jct. Section, Zurich, Blaine Co., Mont." Map dated June 1919, rev. Oct. 1936 and Feb. 1937. Scale 1" = 100', Montana Department of Transportation Collection, Helena.
15. Other towns on the GN in Montana with thirty-by-forty-eight-foot stations were Gildford, Rudyard, Inverness, Joplin (all between Havre and Shelby), Wiota, and Snowden.
16. U.S. Census manuscript returns for Montana, Blaine County, School District No. 17 [Zurich], Jan. 7–14, 1920, microfilm, supplemented by www.ancestry.com.
17. Cushman, *Plenty of Room*, 197.
18. Ibid.
19. Ibid., 193–94.
20. *The Oxford English Dictionary,* 2d ed., vol. 15 (New York: Oxford University Press, 1989), 600. The dictionary reports the earliest appearance of the words in publication in 1905 and 1906.
21. *Official Guide of the Railways,* Jan. 1907, 613, 614, 618.
22. "Correspondence," *The Typographical Journal,* Dec. 1906, 678.
23. Belvina Bertino, *The Man I Knew, The Man I Still Love: A Biography of Frank Lewis Bertino* (Seattle, 1995), 65, quoted in Martha Kohl, *I Do: A Cultural History of Montana Weddings* (Helena, MT: Montana Historical Society Press, 2011), 41.
24. "Skidoo Kid," "Memories of Riding the Great Northern Skidoo," discuss.amtraktrains.com/index.php?/topic/5565-before-amtrak.
25. *Official Guide of the Railways,* July 1956, 1077.
26. *Reports of Cases . . . 1920*, 81–88, quotes on 83–84.
27. Sinclair Lewis, *Free Air* (New York: Harcourt, Brace and Howe, 1919), 87.
28. *Reports of Cases . . . 1920*, 107–23, quotes p. 116. A photo essay on the stations and interchange at Lombard is in "Not on the Highway Maps," *Railroad Magazine,* Oct. 1940, 122–24.
29. Borland, *Country Editor's Boy*, 22, 245, 250, 251, 259–60, 270–71, 277, 283–84, 296–97.
30. Ibid., 313.

Chapter 4

1. John A. Droege, *Passenger Terminals and Trains* (New York: McGraw-Hill Book Company, 1916), 6. Droege emphasizes the eastern United States and terminals in cities much larger than those in Montana.
2. *Official Guide of the Railways,* June 1916, 713.
3. Droege, *Passenger Terminals,* 6.
4. Chicago, Milwaukee & St. Paul Railway, *Passenger Train Schedules, March 1920* (Chicago: Chicago, Milwaukee & St. Paul Railway, 1920), 65–66.
5. U.S. Department of the Interior, National Park Service, National Register of Historic Places Registration Form for "Great Falls Railroad Historic District," prepared by Dena Sanford (May 1992): sect. 8, 9–10.
6. On the relationship between the Northern Pacific and the St. Paul–based architectural firm of Charles Reed and Allen Stem, see Edward W. Nolan, *Northern Pacific Views: The Railroad Photography of F. Jay Haynes, 1876–1905* (Helena, MT: Montana Historical Society Press, 1983), 112, 114.
7. Droege, *Passenger Terminals,* 67, 108.
8. *Butte (MT) Miner,* Aug. 20, 1916, mag. sect., 3.
9. In the 1980s, the author worked for the consulting firm on the second floor.
10. *Official Guide of the Railways,* June 1916, 640, 713.
11. S. Kip Farrington Jr., *Railroading from the Rear End* (New York: Coward McCann, Inc., 1946), 158.
12. *R. L. Polk & Co.'s Livingston City Directory . . . 1916–1917* (Helena, MT: R. L. Polk & Co. of Montana, 1916). Information compiled and extrapolated from the first half of the alphabetical list of names, 33–93.
13. H. Roger Grant, *Railroads and the American People* (Indiana University Press: Bloomington, 2012), 101.
14. *R. L. Polk & Co's Butte City Directory 1917* (Helena, MT: R. L. Polk & Co. of Montana, 1917), 603, 793.
15. Wheeler, *Yankee from the West,* 58–64.
16. *Anaconda (MT) Standard,* Sept. 16, 1906, pt. 2, 1.
17. Ibid., Sept. 11, 1906, 1.
18. *Butte (MT) Miner,* Aug. 13, 1916, ad p. 28.
19. John K. Hutchens, *One Man's Montana: An Informal Portrait of a State* (Philadelphia: J. B. Lippincott Company, 1964), 13–15, 102, 145, 172–73, 177.
20. Ibid., 138–41.

Chapter 5

1. Gil Troy, *See How They Ran: The Changing Role of the Presidential Candidate* (New York: The Free Press, 1991), 190–91.
2. *Montana Standard* (Butte, MT), Feb. 20, 2017, A5, has a list of "Presidential Visits to Montana"—from Chester Arthur in 1883 to Barack Obama in 2009.
3. Craig Reese, "The Gardiner Gateway to Yellowstone," *The Mainstreeter* 15:2 (1996): 6.
4. *Helena (MT) Independent,* Aug. 17, 1892, 4, 8.
5. Troy, *See How They Ran,* 104.
6. William J. Bryan, *The First Battle: A Story of the Campaign of 1896* (Chicago: W. B. Conkey Company, 1896), 619.
7. Charles H. Eggleston, *Anaconda (MT) Standard,* Aug. 13, 1897, in *The Last Best*

Place: A Montana Anthology, ed. William Kittredge and Annick Smith (Helena, MT: Montana Historical Society Press, 1988), 452–55.

8. John M. Hilpert, *American Cyclone: Theodore Roosevelt and His 1900 Whistle-stop Campaign* (Jackson: University Press of Mississippi, 2015), 98–100, 280–81.
9. *Bozeman (MT) Chronicle*, Sept. 12, 1919, 2.
10. *Anaconda (MT) Standard*, July 2, 1923, 1, 4; July 3, 1923, 1.
11. Cushman, *Plenty of Room*, 215.
12. Ibid., 215–16.
13. Ibid., 215.
14. J. Edward Shields, "The Silk Trains," *The Sea Chest: Journal of the Puget Sound Maritime Historical Society* 31:4 (1988): 149.
15. Recalled by Thelma Bruce and Addie Mae Sienknecht in an interview by Dale Martin, July 8, 1982, in Tekoa and paraphrased in Dale Martin, "Tekoa and Malden: A History of Two Railroad Towns in Eastern Washington" (master's thesis, Washington State University, Pullman, 1984), 61–62.
16. *The Montanan, '12* [Montana State College yearbook for the school year 1910–11] (Bozeman, MT, 1911), 78.
17. Wallace Stegner, *Wolf Willow: A History, a Story, and a Memory of the Last Plains Frontier* (New York: Viking Press, 1962); reprint (New York: Penguin Books, 2000), 274.
18. *Bozeman (MT) Chronicle*, Aug. 17, 1892, 4.
19. *Anaconda (MT) Standard*, Oct. 23, 1926, 1, 2; Nov. 19, 1927, 1, 7.
20. *Bozeman (MT) Chronicle*, Oct. 29, 1937, panel ad on p. 4.
21. *Montana Standard* (Butte, MT), Oct. 16, 1948, 1; Oct. 21, 1950, 9.
22. Teresa Jordan, *Riding the White Horse Home: A Western Family Album* (New York: Vintage Books, 1993), 55.
23. Vachel Lindsay, *Adventures while Preaching the Gospel of Beauty* (New York: Macmillan Company, 1921), 48.
24. Ibid., 49–50.
25. Christowe, *My American Pilgrimage*, 199.

Chapter 6

Epigraph: Wendell Berry, *The Long-Legged House* (Washington, DC: Shoemaker & Hoard, 2004), 172.

1. Dan Cushman, *The Grand and the Glorious* (New York: McGraw-Hill Book Company, Inc., 1963), 188.
2. The loss of railroad business to competing modes of transportation, and the roles of both the railroads and the federal government, remain a topic of continuing discussion, controversy, and differing attributions of responsibility. Much of the material in this chapter is derived from the following sources: John F. Stover, *The Life and Decline of the American Railroad* (New York: Oxford University Press, 1970), 192–271; Vance, *Capturing the Horizon*, 485–603; and Mark Reutter, "The Lost Promise of the American Railroad," *The Wilson Quarterly* 18:1 (1994): 10–37. Published in the 1920s, Stuart Daggett's *Principles of Inland Transportation* (New York: Harper & Brothers, 1928) offers early evidence of the rise of competitors to railroads only gradually becoming evident to most outside the transportation business. For example, see pp. 14–16, 100–101, 116–21, 125–26.
3. Meredith Willson, "Rock Island," song from *The Music Man*.
4. *Montana Highway History, Vol. 2: 1943 to 1959* (Helena, MT: Montana State Highway Commission, 1960), 73.

5. *Grit, Guts and Gusto: A History of Hill County* (Havre, MT: Hill County Bicentennial Commission, 1976), 226, 228.
6. Joseph A. Amato, "The Extraordinary Ordinary and the Changing Face of Place," *History News,* Spring 2013, 14.
7. Daggett, *Principles of Inland Transportation,* 14–16.
8. David P. Morgan, "Who Shot the Passenger Train?: Here's What Went Wrong," *Trains,* Apr. 1959, 23.
9. Reutter, "Lost Promise," 23–24.
10. Robert L. Borsos, "Honeymoon Depot," *Trains,* Nov. 2003, 68.
11. *Bozeman (MT) Chronicle,* Oct. 7, 1952, 1, 2.
12. Carol Bradley, "Artistic Setting," *Montana Magazine,* Sept.–Oct. 2014, 22–23.
13. Richard Saunders Jr., *Merging Lines: American Railroads, 1900–1970,* rev. ed. (DeKalb, IL: Northern Illinois University Press, 2001), 109.
14. Ivan Doig, *The Bartender's Tale* (New York: Riverhead Books, 2012), 5.
15. *1961 Montana Highway Map* (Helena, MT: Montana Department of Transportation, 1961); *Official 1971 Highway Map Montana* (Helena, MT: Montana Department of Transportation, 1971).
16. William R. Kuebler, "An Interview with Norm Lorentzen, Part 4–Conclusion: Passenger and Freight Operations," *The Mainstreeter* 13:1 (1994): 15.
17. Kurt E. Armbruster, "The Northern Pacific's Mainstreeter, Part 2: A 'Strange and Curious' Decade," *The Mainstreeter* 17:1 (1998): 18–19.
18. Ralph W. Hidy, Muriel E. Hidy, and Roy V. Scott, with Don L. Hofsommer, *The Great Northern Railway: A History* (Boston: Harvard Business School Press, 1988), 281.
19. Fred W. Frailey, *Twilight of the Great Trains* (Waukesha, WI: Kalmbach Books, 1998), 116.
20. David P. Morgan, "Excuse the First Person," *Trains,* Mar. 1968, 3.
21. Joseph Schwieterman's *When the Railroad Leaves Town: Western United States* examines fifty-eight communities in twenty-five states. Among these are two Montana towns: Harlowton, which until 1980 was a main line division point and junction on the Milwaukee Road, and Red Lodge, which was at the end of an NP branch abandoned in 1981.
22. David Plowden, *Requiem for Steam: The Railroad Photographs of David Plowden* (New York: W. W. Norton & Company, 2010), 9.
23. James L. Ehernberger and Francis G. Gschwind, *Smoke along the Columbia* (Callaway, NE: E. & G. Publications, 1968), 42.
24. Mary Clearman Blew, *Balsamroot: A Memoir* (New York: Viking, 1994), 161.
25. Information compiled from "Montana's Trolleys" series.
26. *Montana Standard* (Butte, MT), Nov. 3, 1929, 29.
27. Thornton H. Waite, "The Passenger Trains of Butte, Montana," *Passenger Train Journal* 237 (Fourth Quarter 2008): 28–29.
28. Taber, "Short Lines of the Treasure State," BA&P chap., 5–8.
29. Craig Sanders, *Amtrak in the Heartland* (Bloomington: Indiana University Press, 2006), 158–66.
30. William Wyckoff, *On the Road Again: Montana's Changing Landscape* (Seattle: University of Washington Press, 2006), 52–53, 148.
31. Stephen B. Goddard, *Getting There: The Epic Struggle between Road and Rail in the American Century* (Chicago: University of Chicago Press, 1996), ix–x, 248. Italics in original.
32. Author's observation, Aug. 26–27, 2006.
33. Dan Machalaba, "What to do about NIMBYs?" *Trains,* Sept. 2010, 44.

34. Northern Plains Resource Council, *The True Cost of Coal Exports: A Report by the Western Organization of Resource Councils and Northern Plains Resource Council* (Billings, MT: NPRC, [2016]), 3.

Conclusion

1. Mary Clearman Blew, *Jackalope Dreams* (Lincoln: University of Nebraska Press, 2008), 89, 265–73, 368–82.
2. *Harlowton (MT) Times-Clarion,* December 6, 2001, 1.

Index

Note: italicized page numbers indicate illustrations or photographs.

ABOUT THE AUTHOR

Dale Martin grew up in Bellevue, Washington, in the Seattle area, and attended Washington State University in Pullman. He has worked in archaeological excavation and survey, historical research, the field study of historic buildings and bridges, and, most recently, teaching history at Montana State University in Bozeman. He has watched and ridden trains on four continents.